PRAISES FOR

Raquel Solomon paints a revealing truth based story. The lies that she has been told are the same lies that we have all heard in our lifetimes. We were waiting with anticipation, to read about how she turned her struggle into triumph.

—Adrena Tolbert, Founder of VEU Magazine

Life is made up of truths and lies. We find common ground in what we choose to believe about ourselves. Raquel paints a beautiful portrait of the importance of believing in yourself above all else.

—JoAnn Jenkins, Writer

An intricately written page turner.

—Alima Albari, CEO Studio Ninety-Two

Lies
MEN
TELL

RAQUEL
SOLOMON

Printed in the United States of America
First Printing, 2017

ISBN: 978-0-9989702-1-9

13th & Joan
500 N. Michigan Avenue, Suite #500
Chicago, IL 60611

WWW.13THANDJOAN.COM

DEDICATION

This book is dedicated to my two beautiful daughters, Taylor Denise Brim and Madison LaRay Lozada. My heart beats for both of you. You have made me such a proud mom. Words cannot explain the love that I have for you.

EPIGRAPH

Love doesn't guarantee a happy ending.

TABLE OF CONTENTS

ACKNOWLEDGEMENTS 9

INTRODUCTION 13

CHAPTER 1: A FALSE START......................................17

CHAPTER 2: THE WONDER YEARS...........................31

CHAPTER 3: BLOOD IS THICKER THAN WATER 43

CHAPTER 4: CALIFORNIA DREAMIN' 57

CHAPTER 5: A DIFFERENT POINT OF VIEW..............67

CHAPTER 6: THE PIECES OF ME 85

CHAPTER 7: THE BEST THING YOU NEVER HAD 99

CHAPTER 8: NEVER SAY NEVER............................115

CHAPTER 9: WOMAN, THOU ART LOOSED 131

CHAPTER 10: EXPECT THE UNEXPECTED 145

CHAPTER 11: AND NOW, I'LL DO
WHAT'S BEST FOR ME 154

EPILOGUE 163

ABOUT THE AUTHOR...167

ACKNOWLEDGEMENTS

First, I would like to thank my Lord and Savior Jesus Christ, for without you, none of this would be possible. You have taught me so many things through this thing called life, most importantly how to trust and depend on you and only you. You have carried me during my weakest time and taught me the importance of being still when I was moving too fast. Thank you for keeping my children and me safe and our hearts happy and full of love.

My daddy, I thank you for teaching me how to be independent, how to cook the most difficult meal, and most importantly, for loving me unconditionally. My first job was working for you in your upholstery shop and it was there where I learned how to be professional and work with people. You are the best daddy any girl could ever ask for. You are truly amazing and now I understand why you have always had so many friends. I love you more than all the words, in all the books, in all the world.

Mama, I will just keep it "real" and thank you for teaching me not to take any shit from anyone. Because of you, I learned never to let anyone disrespect me and to fire back if someone takes a jab. Through your wisdom, I have cultivated the art of fighting with silence. You educated me about the finer things, and now I am able to take care of and appreciate the things I have. Between you and daddy, I think you produced a pretty well rounded daughter.

Debbie and Lisa, I thank you for being an example and teaching me, "your little sister," how to be a young lady. Thank you for your protection and love.

Taylor and Madison, thank you for being God-fearing and loving young ladies. You have encouraged me, taught me, and supported me through my endeavors. I thank God for picking me to be your mom. I love you both, always and forever.

Aunt Elaine (President) and Aunt Mart (Vice President), you two have always been my foundation. I have looked up to you since the Rock Child Chip days. You were always there for me when I needed to talk to someone. You are two of the most amazing women that I have ever known. I love you both and thank you for always showing me love.

Traci and Monica, thank you cousins for being down since day one. We three have been through it and I love you both so much. Traci, thank you for taking me in to live with you when I first moved to Sacramento. Those Lincoln Village days made us strong. Monica — girl — where do I begin? You and I have cried so many tears and in the same hour, jumped in our car, blasting Mary J Blige, and demanding respect from whoever came our way. We were some bad bitches back in the day. I love you both so much and am so thankful for your love and friendship.

Thank you 13th & Joan for believing in my story, and having faith in me to publish my novel. Ardre Orie, aka Queen, thank you for the new found friendship. You are such a badass chick! I have another book ready for you.

If you have been a part of my life and helped, listened to me, coached, guided, supported me, or just prayed for me, I thank you from the bottom of my heart. I love you all.

INTRODUCTION

*"The truth may hurt for a little while,
but the pain of lies is everlasting."*

My name is Raquel and I solemnly swear to tell the truth, the whole truth, and nothing but the truth. And if it's the truth sets us free, then I'd say that I'm running as fast as I can towards the promised land. Up until this point, my whole life has been plagued by lies — lies men tell to be exact.

Although this entire book is based on lies, I promise you that I will get as close to the truth that you need to know as possible. You see, I live my life today anchored in truth and I'll admit that sometimes the real truth is too much for some to bear. The events that have transpired in my life make me walk the tightrope of truth every second, of every minute, of every hour of the day. My life's experiences have taught me that the truth is the only thing that I can firmly stand on when the titanic of life sinks. I used to thrive in the flames of lies that we so often tell ourselves. We tell lies to be accepted, we believe lies to be truths we wish existed, and we accept lies because we don't often feel worthy of better.

It took me quite some time to figure out the difference, but now I know; truth is not always what we want, it doesn't weigh us down with guilt and haunt us in our private hours the way that lies do.

I must have started and stopped writing this book at least twenty times because I didn't want to hurt people or challenge anyone else's reality with what I now know to be the truth and the many revelations that I have gleaned along the way. I've waited so long to tell the truth that it almost suffocated me. Today, I walk boldly in my decision to share my journey with you. You need to know.

The most compelling force that gave me the strength to document my truths in a way that would forever be memorialized was the fact that I have been misunderstood so much throughout my life. It is my belief that I have been understood by few and misunderstood by many.

I never quite realized that what I searched for so desperately was disguised in truth. I decided to come forward with the truth, because I knew that if I could share with you a complete look at my losses and triumphs and how I managed to overcome them, you could find the strength to do so too. Today, I'm brutally honest about everything in my life and while I do believe some things should be kept private, I also know how therapeutic it can be to release the truth. In truth, I discovered a freedom that most never get to experience in a lifetime. This freedom is the key to the fountain of youth and the answer on how to live life more abundantly. If my truth helps one woman or man then without question, I have succeeded.

I no longer worry about what others will say, or how they will feel, because the truth is just that, truth. In this lifetime, the truth is what we will have left to stand on when everything else perishes. The truth becomes the legacy that you never knew existed. The truth represents the seams that are sown together to bind the quilt of your life.

No longer will I be bound by lies. I'm a walking, talking, lie detector test. Ha! I've heard just about every lie there ever was to be told. The question, I often ask myself is, why was I so willing to listen to the lies told by men? What truth did I seek in the sea of lies told to me? As women, we must find a place of understanding within ourselves to dissect the lies that we accept.

Let's be clear, this is not a story written to bash men because women tell lies too. I've just come to realize that women deserve to know the real truths and the reasons why lies become such a big part of who we become and what we accept. Now that I have your attention, journey with me along a road paved with the haze of a desire for true love.

1: A FALSE START

"Every new beginning is the result of an end."

Meeting someone new and falling in love is one of life's greatest gifts, especially for a hopeless romantic like me. I have always believed in love and I will continue to believe. There is no force more powerful than the beating of our hearts when it yearns for another. The power to touch, to feel, and to live is equivalent to breath for me. I love, love.

Over the years, I've had to ask myself, if love will ever be willing to love me back. Like every face, I too have a story to tell. So much of what has happened in my life was a result of my searching for the very essence of who I was, and repeated questioning of my identity. I was born Rachel Dene' Larson. Even as a baby, the plan for me was not clearly defined. When my mother brought me home from the hospital, she hadn't yet named me. Small, yet meaningful details like this would plague me such that I would not know how to recognize who I was, or what I wanted as I grew older. Today, as I reflect on my life, there are not many pictures or traces of my childhood. I always wondered if there was a special blueprint for my life. I seemed to live in a constant state of change, sometimes forwards and sometimes backwards, but always a different direction. I eventually decided to create my own path, but not without resistance, heartbreak, and sometimes even turmoil. That's what happens when you are just trying to find your way. If you have no intended destination, any road will take you there.

Today, my destination is crystal clear and although every aspect of my journey is not planned, nor do I believe it should be, I do have an intended destination and I am clear about who I want to be when I get there. I am a firm believer that to truly understand where you are going, you must know where you've been. So, let's go back to the beginning.

LIE #1: YOUR PAST HAS NOTHING TO DO WITH YOUR FUTURE.

As much as I'd like to believe that our pasts and our futures are not connected, I must admit that this notion is one of many lies. I told you that I was going to tell you the truth, the whole truth, and nothing but the truth, no matter how hard it becomes. I could go on for days telling you about the men in my life, and believe me I will, but to truly understand why I made some of the decisions that I made, I have to teach you about who I am, my motivations, and the way in which I grew up. These things undeniably make us who we are and easily serve as indicators of what we will become.

I could never forget the number 150. 150 Churchill Lane was home for us. Our house was situated towards the back of the subdivision. There was only one way in and one way out and because the neighborhood was so close to the freeway, it was never quiet. Our home was the most noticeable in the neighborhood with its golden yellow hue. I felt like I could spot our house from a mile away, even while riding home on the school bus. Back then, I remembered getting off the bus and walking towards the house. As I would approach our home, the yellow reminded me of sunshine. That same sunshine was also felt inside. No matter what happened in our lives, my home was filled with love. 150 was a three bedroom, one bathroom house, with a detached garage, and boy did that garage take on a life of its own. It was never empty, as it was home to my dad's upholstery business. There were always nails, and tacks, and sharp objects on the ground, and just outside of the garage was parked our Ford Gran Torino

There was a big bay window at the front of the house. When you entered the home, you became a witness to a hodgepodge of real life. Everything from the huge fish aquarium, to the protruding wall heater, was visible. Our bedrooms were situated towards the rear of the home and the small, but functional, kitchen was always inhabited by my mother or father cooking. I have so many memories of the backyard. It was always filled with cars and upholstery materials. I spent hours out there playing with my dolls and looking for ladybugs on the side of the house. I could always see the chain-link fence from my peripheral view between the neighbors and our home. Did I mention that our garage was a disaster? Well, it was. Upholstery supplies were everywhere. You had to wear shoes or you were liable to step on a nail and that meant excruciating pain. Trust me, I know from experience.

My sisters and I would live for the moments when we could pick from the loquat tree. Its yellow berry appearance made it so appealing. It looked like a sweet piece of fruit and it was. When loquat season hit, everyone would come over to pick from our tree. My sister would say, "There's some loquats on the tree," and I would be responsible for getting a bag to collect them. We never even washed them before eating them. No one cared about that back then. We lived in the moment. It was the same with the trees that grew the little deep red plums.

Open invitations were a staple with our family, but it didn't stop real life from taking place. If you opened the door on any given day, my mother could be found fussing. She was always fussing about something. She was always irritated. She wasn't an, "I love you!" type of mother. Never one for too many words, but we knew that she loved us. As a child, I could sense that she wasn't happy with herself. It's amazing that from a young age, I picked up on that. I'm not even sure that she knew how much she had going for herself.

My mother was so beautiful. She was a mix between the legendary singers Lena Horne and Sade. She had long hair and would always wear it pulled back into a ponytail. She also had a beautiful shape. I always understood why my dad wanted to marry her. She wore very little makeup. She didn't have a need for it. Sometimes, she would go to her girlfriend's house and she would get her hair bleached, but it was always very classy. Her taste overall was impeccable, but she also had immaculate taste in material things. Our mailbox would be filled with Neiman Marcus and Bloomingdale's catalogs. With her, I observed the finer things. I would flip through the catalogs and admire the beautiful wine glasses. I always thought to myself, "If I save a dollar every day, I could get one glass." She had over three hundred pairs of shoes. Even back then, she was wearing Charles Jourdan, which was like the Christian Louboutin of today. She wasn't materialistic, but she wanted quality. If there were two sets of glasses, she wanted the ones that were crystal. During that time, my mom worked at Convair Pioneer

Hospital, a convalescent hospital for adults. She got off of work at half past three and sometimes my dad would take me to go and pick her up. There were eight-foot high gates surrounding the building and occasionally there would be adult patients standing outside. In retrospect, it was a mental hospital, but the way in which the patients that stood outside acted, made me question how crazy the patients inside were.

I think that my mom's work is what caused her to often feel unhappy. Her job was tough and to see people in a state of what appeared to be disarray could take a toll. She wasn't affectionate, and although we knew that she loved us, it was implied more than shown. My father's face, however, revealed a different story. He could be found on any given day, standing over the stove cooking. He was always cooking. He taught us that it didn't have to be a holiday to eat chitlins, collard greens, and black-eyed peas. He'd say, "I got three bunches of greens in the kitchen. I am going to give you five dollars to clean them." He even taught us how to make fried chicken as early as the fourth grade. He would cook and eat rattlesnake soup and turtle soup and he learned to eat "city bird" from his mom, Flauna Bell. City bird is a bird that you find dead on the street. He ate so many strange foods that I thought that if he ever died it would be from food poisoning. He ate, quite literally, everything.

More than anything, Daddy was really into upholstery work. There were always upholstery books everywhere in the house. They were on the kitchen table, in the living room, and even in the bathroom. His passion took over everything. How many people can say they have a button maker in their house? Well I could.

People would bring their cars over to have their seats upholstered, but Dad would never just let them drop their cars off, he would also cook them a meal. He was liked by so many people and was so friendly. When we had visitors, whether they were his clients or friends, he never made us go into our rooms. He would allow us to be a part of the conversation. We enjoyed his company. It was always a learning experience.

Behind my father's smile, there was also pain. He was a functioning alcoholic. His alcoholism affected the family dynamic but not in ways that you would imagine. It turned him into a merry partier. He would sometimes fall asleep in the middle of the floor and my mother would get so upset, but in all honesty, we had so much fun with him and so did the community. He had white friends, Chinese friends, African friends, friends from all ethnicities. No one was ever a stranger for long and everyone loved him.

When I was born, my dad was an entrepreneur. He stood about five foot, nine inches, with beautiful brown skin. His smile was always captivating. He had such a jovial personality. Besides owning the upholstery business, he was also a campus supervisor, or narc, which is a yard duty person. When I was in the third grade, he worked at Tehachapi State Prison, located in California, about forty minutes outside of Bakersfield. He worked there as a vocational instructor, focusing on upholstery for level three inmates. This job validated what he had done for so many years. It gave him a regular paycheck, for which he didn't have to solicit, and though he worked with high-level inmates, he never really encountered any problems. Dad's personality lended itself toward creating cohesiveness.

My father was very easy to talk to. I know now that I had adopted his personality. I understood the importance of being kind to people. Growing up, I never knew one person that didn't like him. He was so charismatic and loving that you could never tell if he didn't care for someone. Not liking people was never a subject of discussion with him. He was always giving. It seemed as though he got more energy from giving of himself to others. It was a quality that I most admired about him.

Even though my father was easygoing, there was something about the interactions that he and my mother shared that made their relationship volatile. It was almost as if they were oil and water. My mother could not stand the fact that my dad was an alcoholic. She would hit him, without justification, when he was drunk and I didn't like it. I felt like he was so vulnerable and it made me dislike her. It still hurts my heart to this day to remember those times. There were times that I believe my mother found it hard to turn off her work persona and turn on her home persona. Sometimes, I felt like she talked to us as if we were patients at the hospital. Her communication skills were very poor and my father's disposition angered her. There was a heaviness that she carried around and it was recognizable by anyone who met her. Now, looking back, I can't imagine what it was like to have worked under the conditions that she did. I believe that shopping became her escape. When I moved out the house, she had over two thousand pairs of shoes.

I never quite understood how my parents hit it off. How did they decide to get married? How did they even date? I've never in my entire life seen them kiss or hold hands. I've never heard them say, "I love you," to each other. These factors affected my perception of relationships and my disposition in them.

KENTON AND MARIETTA

Kenton and Marietta are my mother's parents. They were married in a small city near Bakersfield and soon after had my mother, Morgan and my Uncle, Lenton. Their marriage wasn't a happy one. Kenton never liked my mom and when I was very young, he left for the store and never came back. It was disturbing for everyone. My dad went searching for him, but my grandfather wasn't to be found. Marietta, who I called Momma Mary, eventually remarried. Her husband was named Chance, but I would forever know him as my grandfather, Charlie.

I would stay with Momma Mary and Charlie every summer. They were both very good to me. Momma Mary was an alcoholic like my father and a hypochondriac like my mother, but Charlie was a big man like Santa Claus, with a round belly and a beautiful head of salt and pepper hair. His biggest vice was smoking cigars and pipes and I remember fondly our trips to the tobacco shop.

My childhood summer memories are filled with many loving recollections. It's funny the things that stand out that are forever cemented in our minds. I remember Charlie's favorite meal was Shake N Bake pork chops. I also remember the crochet classes Momma Mary signed me up for. Even more, I recall her powder blue, crushed velvet couch in the living room, the immaculate way she kept her beautiful house, and the Koi pond in the backyard. However, it was their relationship and the way they treated one another that truly stood out. They were, quite simply, good together and they became my blueprint for what a marriage should be.

Charlie was a construction worker and he would leave really early every morning. Together, Momma Mary and I would make coffee for him and then keep him company, sitting at the table while he put on his work boots. Later, after a long day of work, I would be at the front window, waiting for him to return.

"Momma Mary, Charlie is home," I'd yell in excitement.

He would sit on a chair in the garage and take off his work boots. Mama Mary, being a very traditional wife, cooked him a hot meal every day. Sometimes, she would even let me help her cook. The meals were an important part of their day. It helped them stay connected.

Kenton never resurfaced and I think that my mother's childhood greatly affected the way in which she loved my father and us. Had Charlie come into her life sooner, she might not have had such a recipe of issues, but the dysfunction carried over into our home. What's worse is that both my grandmother and Kenton passed away before she was able to get any closure on the matter.

FLAUNA BELL & CLIFTON

Flauna Bell and Clifton were my father's parents. I called Flauna, "Grandmomie". She was a big lady, standing at about five foot nine and would best be described as solid. She had a beauty shop adjacent to her house and it seemed like all of the old ladies in Bakersfield came to her place to get their hair done. She made her own grease, an ointment for the hair, and she would add peppermint to it, so when everyone was getting their hair pressed the room smelled fresh.

I never had the chance to meet my grandfather, Clifton. He passed away before I was born, but my sisters knew him and told me stories of "Paw Paw," the loving nickname they had given him. What I learned of Paw Paw was that he had dearly loved my mother and would have done anything for her. I believe that together, Grandmomie and Paw Paw gave my mom the love that her own parents hadn't given her.

Besides being a hairdresser, Grandmomie was also an amazing cook. She would bake cookies for us all the time. We later learned that she had not been replacing the cookies in the jar with the fresh ones. The new ones were set on the top, but the old ones that had not been consumed, over time lined the bottom. The joke was, "Who is going to eat Grandmomie's cookies?"

There is a treasure trove of memories from spending time at my Grandmomie's home. I remember picking all of the grapes off the vine that grew on the side of her house, and then joking with my cousin, Tracy about opening a winery. I know that there was a Loquat tree and a few apple trees that grew on the property. Grandmomie would pick up the apples from the ground and put them out on the table for eating even though they had worms in them. I recall the days spent pickling and canning food and the outhouse where she kept everything. It was always filled with pickles and cha cha (a hot relish spread with peppers and hot sauce). Every Christmas, Grandmomie would make a fruitcake. She would put dates and raisins in it and then wrap it beautifully. Then, sadly, she would serve it to us kids and we absolutely hated it. We would run into the backyard saying, "Ew!

Are you going to eat that?" We knew the reason behind her frugal ways and her less than "kid friendly" eating habits. Her grandparents had been slaves and she had been raised to waste nothing.

Her one bad habit was dipping snuff, which looked like a chocolate brownie. She would sit in her chair and hold her "spit cup". Every so often, when she placed the spit cup beside her chair, it would accidentally spill and it smelled horrible. My cousins and I always exchanged laughs and would dare each other to take a bite of her snuff brownie. I'm not sure if anyone ever took the dare.

More than anything, I remember the very active role Grandmomie had in all of our lives. We would sit on her lap, hug her, and knew she would always be available to us. If I had to describe her with one word, it would be loving. She never once beat us, or mistreated us, and for that, we will forever be grateful.

DAWN & LYNN

Dawn and Lynn are my sisters. As youngsters, they resembled each other so much that they were often mistaken as twins. Lynn has a very fair complexion and she reminds me of Grandmomie. In her youth, she had long, flowing hair and was somewhat of a tomboy. All of her friends were boys from the neighborhood. She was a fighter in school and honey, let me tell you, she was bad to the bone; never letting anything overtake her. She started abusing alcohol in the eighth grade, but still managed to graduate with honors during her sophomore year of high school, though no one ever knew. She just took life by the horns.

Dawn is older and eventually, we formed a close bond. It took a while to establish that connection as her disposition, just out of high school, changed. It took time, but as we got older, we leaned on one another and to this day, we share a love for parenting.

In essence, I have become the by-product of every single family member that came before me. I believe that we all do. Even so, I was still in search of the attributes that would set me apart and those that would define me. There is no denying that the love of family was ever present. I also couldn't deny the fact that I wanted more. My adolescent years, like many, would find me searching for love outside of my immediate family. I knew that it existed and I wanted to experience it for myself. This search, as I now call it, would lead me to places unknown, some good and some bad, but none without valuable lessons that I would come to recognize as truths.

2: THE WONDER YEARS

"Being loved gives you courage, loving gives you strength."

As much as I wanted to believe that the love I sought at such a young age was in search of me, that was a lie. I was searching for love. The wonder years often lead you to discover love in peculiar places. These years can best be described as a mix between tender and experimental in nature. Very often, there is no evidence of destruction or reckless behavior and in consideration, very little apprehension. The wonder years as I have often heard them referred to, make you do just that — wonder. Upon reflection, you often wonder what you were thinking, if you were thinking at all; and how life would have unfolded differently if you had possessed the ability to heed foreshadowing. There is admittedly a reverence for this period in your life and as reckless as it may have been, it was all a meticulous venture of innocence.

LIE #2: PEOPLE CAN CHANGE.

How do you remember your first day of high school? I imagine most of you felt jitters and butterflies, not me. I don't recall feeling nervous because I had friends from my neighborhood attending the same school. I didn't feel lost as many describe. What I do remember, is the presence of what appeared to be selective segregation. On that first day, I stood from a distance and watched as my friends of various colors divided themselves, whites with whites and blacks with blacks. But, where was I to go? I was friends with everyone and had never even considered separating myself. I had come from a home where we embraced everyone. I had watched as my father invited people of every color into our home and cooked for them. Up until that day, I hadn't realized that racism and being separate was really a thing.

There was a tree that was referred to as the "Nigga Tree." All the people under that tree were being bussed in and that group in my opinion seemed a little too aggressive for my liking. The alternative was where my white friends congregated, but now cognizant of the differences, I didn't recognize anyone there whom I could relate to. It was a very weird space to be in. I'll admit that I felt alone.

Most of the blacks who stood under the Nigga Tree lived in what we referred to as, the country, and I wasn't from there. I saw nothing wrong with either group; I just didn't fit in on either side. I wasn't black enough, or as lively, as the people with whom I shared the same skin color, and I clearly was not white. I didn't want to be like anyone else. I just wanted to be me. In the midst of confusion and slight bewilderment, I found a nearby bench to sit on. It was one of the few empty spaces, as the students were everywhere and clearly excited.

While sitting there, my friend Shannay passed by and began to talk with me. It eased my thoughts and took my mind to another place. In the middle of her sentence, she turned around and yelled out, "Peter." She began waving her hand in excitement and she took off running towards the school parking lot. I was left alone again, or so I thought. Shannay turned around and ran back, reaching out the same hand that she had been waving with and said, "Come on girl, let's go." Hand in hand, I ran with her towards the parking lot. I had no idea where we were going or who Peter was. As we got closer, I saw him. I'm not sure if he noticed me, but I most certainly noticed him.

Peter stood about six feet tall with chocolate skin, the kind that glistened in the sunlight. As we got closer, I noticed that his heart shaped smile served as the perfect backdrop to his white teeth. I still can't shake that feeling when I see a chocolate man with a Colgate smile. It just does something to me, and I guess Peter is where it all began. It wasn't love at first sight and yet, how was I to know that my sitting on the bench the first day at school, trying to decipher where I fit in, would lead to meeting someone that I would eventually fall madly and deeply in love with? How was I to know that I was looking at what would be my introduction to love? I didn't. I couldn't. Shannay stopped running in haste and extended her free arm towards the car to break our speed. She introduced me to Peter formally and I could tell from their exchange that they were friends from the past. As they spoke, I fidgeted with my nails, peeling away some of the old pink polish that had begun to chip. I had painted one coat too many the night before.

I noticed that Peter stood with his legs crossed, one in front of the other in full confidence. His car, a dull, Pepto Bismol pink, Volkswagen Bug, was not feminine, although it wouldn't have mattered because he was clearly certain of his manhood. He was so masculine with his movements and the way in which he spoke. He was smooth, I'll admit. Truth moment: He was nice to look at, but I was even more drawn to his car. It was a convertible and I was intrigued. While Peter and Shannay continued to talk, I closed my eyes and envisioned myself behind the wheel. It was wrapped in black leather and I had never seen a car like that before, not even in my dad's upholstery garage.

"Let's go," said Shannay. Without hesitation, I hopped in the back and Shannay took the passenger seat. We had no idea where he would take us and in retrospect, I don't think we really cared. As we cruised, I allowed the California breeze to soothe me. I forgot all about feeling out of place at school; in that moment I felt free and my mind was at ease. I remember lifting my arms to the heavens and gazing up at the sun. I found myself in the midst of a happy place and like something out of a typical romantic comedy, while I was caught up in the mystique, swept off my feet, reality decided to slap me right in the face. As I gazed into the clouds that were playing hide and seek with the sun, something flew into my eye and the pain was almost too great to bear. Peter had to pull the car over due to my yelling and screaming for help. Thankfully, Shannay, with the help of a water bottle from her backpack, was able to flush out my eye. I should have taken that as a sign that nothing from that moment forward would go according to plan. I should have, but I didn't.

Peter suggested that we head back to the school as not to be late. When we arrived, Shannay hopped out and turned around to release the seat so that I could step out of the back. Just as I placed my foot onto the sidewalk, I felt Peter touch my hand. He had written his number on a piece of paper to give to me. He didn't say, "Call me," or "I want to see you again," or anything for that matter. He just smiled and turned towards the steering wheel preparing to put the car back in drive. I got out, placed his number in the front pocket of my backpack, and took off running hand in hand with Shannay back towards the school. As we got closer, our jog turned into a speed walk. I turned around and looked back at Peter. He was still sitting there in his car. He hadn't driven off so hastily after all. He was still looking at us and he waved goodbye. I was a little taken aback wondering if he was that sure of himself, and that sure that I would even be interested in him. It was awfully presumptuous of him to assume that I would call. Was he that amazing? Regardless, he seemed to personify a confidence that I had never seen before. He was intriguing and I wanted to learn more.

That first day of school was somewhat of a haze, but I remember realizing that he didn't actually attend the school. He had only been in the parking lot to pick up girls in his car, and that day he only got one.

Peter began calling immediately. My mom was very opposed to it. Like most mothers of adolescent daughters, she just did not want me to have a boyfriend. Peter was charming and charismatic and ultimately , he found ways to win her over. I will never forget that she needed her kitchen painted, and oh boy, that was his in.

When I was growing up, if a boy was visiting me, he had to come over, sit in the open, and watch TV with the rest of the family. He had to sit in one chair and I had to sit in another. My parents didn't play. Peter was made to adhere to those rules and he did. Eventually, the courting process turned into us dating formally.

Peter, after a while, took me to his house to meet his family. His home was quite a distance away from mine as he lived in the country, where the kids who stood under the Nigga Tree had been bussed in from. To say I was nervous would be a gross understatement. My armpits told the story. As much as I'd like to, I will never forget the rings of sweat that made their presence known on my pink blouse. It was as if I had Niagara Falls under my armpits. I didn't know much about Peter's family other than he had several siblings, many of whom were adults still living at home with their parents. They were an extremely tight knit family and the children reverenced their parents with uncompromising respect.

Peter's family home felt alive to me. Although nothing was out of place, everything reflected the experiences of the lives that had been lived there. The pillows on the sofa were just worn enough, the edges of the carpet were raised slightly, and if you looked hard enough, you could see fine scuff marks on the walls where hands had once rested. This was not a house; it was a home, a family home; a place that had seen blood, sweat and tears over many generations. It was their safe haven. Despite the relaxed and warm feeling of the home, my armpits continued their waterworks.

Instead of going into the living room to sit with everyone like we had done at my house, we went straight to his mom and dad's bedroom. It was where everyone congregated, the epicenter of their home. Peter guided me to an old, muted, mustard colored chair, with a high back, and wooden trim. I sat, listened, and observed as they all talked. Their exchange showed that they were simply happy to be in each other's presence. It was beautiful to witness and I wanted to be part of it. To me it felt like true love. The longer I stayed, the more comfortable I felt, though my nerves never quite settled. Peter's twin sisters included me right off and though I didn't add much to the conversation they were both very kind to me. As his mother began to speak, one of the sisters fell to the floor and began to shake uncontrollably. I was frightened to say the least. She seemed fine only moments before and now there was a buzzing sound coming from her mouth. She had fallen just close enough to my foot that I could feel her body convulsing. I didn't know what to do, how to react, or if I should be helping her in some way. Peter's family, however, remained calm and his father came over to hold her. I heard them mention something about making sure that she did not swallow her tongue. I never even knew that was possible. The whole situation was shocking. Eventually, she stopped and regained her composure though she continued to lay on the floor in her father's arms. Their ability to remain at ease and yet be closely attentive should probably have alleviated the fear I was feeling, but it only made me more aware of it. So much for first impressions. I felt like I was failing miserably. Trying to focus on something else, I concentrated on Peter's father. He sat close to me while holding his daughter and I noticed his brown skin. Peter's complexion and body type was similar though his father was lighter.

Once Peter recognized that his sister would be OK, he invited me to walk outside. I couldn't have been more relieved. I wasn't sure if my shirt was completely soaked at this point, but fresh air was exactly what I needed.

As we walked towards the back of their home, Peter explained that his sister suffered from epilepsy. He went on to tell me that they had all been trained in how to be of assistance, if necessary and that it was not life threatening. As we circled the house, I noticed that new rooms had been added to the home by his father, on what looked like several different occasions. Possibly, it had been done to accommodate all of the adult children that lived there. Peter invited me to sit with him on a huge crate positioned near a fence. I was surprised at first that it held our weight, but he knew his environment.

"Hey, you want to hold something," he asked.

"What is it?" I asked carefully. I didn't want to hold a snake or anything creepy. He hopped off the crate and walked into a shed. It looked dark inside so I decided not to follow him. As he emerged, I could see that smile and those teeth that had drawn me in from the beginning. He was holding a huge cage that revealed a white bunny. It was beautiful, with the silkiest looking fur I had ever seen. I was so excited and couldn't wait to hold it in my arms.

Peter set the cage on the ground right in front of the crate and said, "Go ahead." As soon as I stuck my hand into the cage, the bunny bit my finger ferociously. I snatched my hand back, counted to make sure all my fingers were still there and saw that the wound was bleeding. Peter consoled me and took me to a nearby water hose to wash the blood away. He was caring and considerate and I liked what I felt when I was with him. And even though my day seemed like an endless culmination of embarrassing events — my shirt never recovered by the way — being with Peter and getting to know him better made it all worthwhile.

We continued our walk and I learned more about the country life he and his family lived. They had several animals at their place; the usual dogs, cats and a few scattered chickens, but after the bunny incident, I steered clear of the lot of them, especially the dogs. It was only later that I learned the bunny was in fact the most dangerous of the group. None of the dogs had any teeth. The day ended, but my love with Peter was just beginning.

Peter continued bringing me around his family. We had a little more privacy at his home than at mine, and it gave us the freedom to experiment the way that teenagers do. Our level of affection for each other grew, but it was over an extended period of time. Nothing is rushed in the country.

Even with the privacy, there were always people around at Peter's home. With all of his siblings and his parents and the many different schedules, the house never truly slept. His mother was always frying chicken and fish and they made a point to enjoy family meals together. I grew increasingly fond of spending time with them. Peter's mother was of the traditional Apostolic faith. They believed in speaking in tongues, prayer, and the Holy Ghost. All of Peter's sisters wore dresses, never pants and little lace doilies over their hair.

Despite our religious differences, they always extended open arms to me and I felt very much a part of his family as the months passed. I found that I wanted to be more like them. I admired how Peter's parents had set expectations for their children, no matter how old they were. There was structure in their house that I had not experienced in my own home. It was also made crystal clear that respect was not optional, but essential. Although this country life was totally different from mine, I embraced it fully and it embraced me back.

Peter had a job at McDonalds, working the Big Mac Grill. Thinking that it would be a way for us to spend more time together and also make some money of my own, I applied for a job and upon acceptance, was trained as a cashier. I enjoyed the responsibility and it was fun taking orders and working the shake machine. Still, I found myself continuously glancing over my shoulder to catch Peter's eye, and just like clockwork, he would flash that smile that drove me crazy. We didn't need to exchange words. Those little moments seemed to further cement our affection for one another.

Eleven months had passed since Peter and I first met and I was happy about the direction that our relationship was headed in. I didn't quite know the final destination but I did know that we were amazing friends and more was on the horizon. I was falling deeply for him. New chapters were preparing to be written and new life would continue to blossom.

3: BLOOD IS THICKER THAN WATER

"It is very possible for two hearts to have only one thing in mind."

Do you believe that it is ever really possible to know all that there is to know about a person? It is my belief that we learn about those who we allow to enter our lives in seasons. After the initial season ends, so does the honeymoon phase and you are granted access to another layer. Layer by layer and bit by bit, you are introduced to who you thought you already knew. The truth is that life has to unravel at the seams for you to learn who someone really is.

LIE #3: WHAT YOU SEE IS WHAT YOU GET.

After spending so much time with Peter and his family, I felt honored to be a part of his world. His presence and my place within his family became one of my fondest memories of my high school years. I believed that our love was a fairy tale unfolding before my eyes, but I was young and naive and didn't realize how much was left to be desired. For all the good that existed within, Peter also had a bad side that was becoming noticeable and recognizable. I learned that he had dropped out of high school and that he was selling drugs on the street corners. My time at his home had increased, but his presence there had decreased. He would leave me with his parents while he made his runs. I kept my grades up at school, maintaining a 3.8 GPA, and to any onlooker I appeared to be a normal teenager. But I was caught between the life I knew, growing up in the west coast suburbs, and the life that I was weaving together with Peter in the country. I knew what he was doing and never attempted to tell him otherwise. In essence, I inadvertently became an assistant to his operations. I never touched any drugs, but I supported him, which meant that I was also accepting his actions. Peter had won my parents over. They saw how good he was to me and accepted our friendship. Although it was never stated that we were dating, they were not in the dark about what was happening. I was, overall, a good girl who made excellent grades and got into very little trouble, so they saw no harm in my spending time with Peter.

While at school one day, I met a young lady named Inglesia. I can't even recall how I met her. I guess she recognized something in me that she saw in herself. We spoke often and she became a confidant. Like me, she also dated an older boy who did not attend the school and who sold drugs. His name was Mark.

She would always say, "Girl, you don't want to take a little bit of that for yourself?"

Basically implying that I should take some of Peter's money and put it away for myself. I guess I could understand her train of thought, but I just didn't have to. Peter took great care of me in that respect. If there was ever anything that I wanted or needed, he didn't hesitate. He never just handed over money to me, but there wasn't anything that I ever went without. Not to mention, I was with Peter for who he was. I had fallen for him without ever even knowing that he sold drugs or had access to excessive money. On many occasions, Peter would give me money and I would go buy groceries to bring back to his home. His mother would cook and I would sometimes assist. I regularly took plates of food to Peter while he worked on the street. He mostly frequented the corner of Lotus Land and Cottontree Road. I knew that what he was doing was wrong, but every moment with his family felt so right. Between all of his sisters, brothers, nieces and nephews, his father's love, and his mother's constant teachings about God, a hole in my soul was filled. Even at a young age, I'm not sure that I could have verbalized it. All I knew was that being with them felt right. Most importantly, Peter had become my best friend. At school, I didn't quite have a place where I belonged, but with him, I did.

Even though I felt that meeting him was a blessing, I can now admit that it was also a curse. I began to hate school. The more I went, the more I wanted to be with Peter. Our relationship became emotional and physical and I gave myself to him. He was the first. It was just another layer of our relationship. Even after our first times together, he never treated me differently. We were in love.

His car was an escape for us. We would take off for a ride whenever the mood hit and when the sun went down we would stop at the local, highly frequented Century Park and make the windows fog up. I remember one evening in particular when a light was shined into the car. It was the police and we were scrutinized for making out in the back seat. They told us to go home and we obeyed so as not to get into any further trouble. During my senior year, this behavior became more regular, but rather than the park, we would go to hotels to get away and be alone. We not only enjoyed each other's company, but we also enjoyed the physical relationship that we shared. The various rooms of the Motel 6 became our regular love nest. We never engaged at his house as his parents were always there and even though his room was way in the back, it didn't offer enough privacy for the level of engagement that we now were involved in.

During this same time, I was involved in an accident while out with my parents in which I fell and hit my head. I suffered a concussion and from this, I developed chronic migraines. Sometimes, while at Peter's home, his mother would take me into the living room and lay me down on the sofa where she would pray profusely and repeatedly for me. To my surprise, the pressure from the headache would often be relieved. This was when I discovered the power of prayer. It seemed to be the only thing that worked. I remember expressing to my own mother how Peter's mom relieved my headaches, but I don't think that she actually believed me. Small, but very meaningful difference between his family and mine were impactful for me.

I was eager to graduate and begin a new chapter. I hated school more and more each day. Dating an older guy excluded me from many of the social events that everyone was so eager to participate in. During senior year, most girls were looking forward to prom, grad night, and senior bash. I didn't have those things to look forward to. Peter wasn't excited about them because he had dropped out of school years previously. To make up for the traditional activities I missed out on, Peter would arrange for us to do nice things together when special school events happened. He took me on a trip to see my sisters in the Bay Area and other times we went out for a nice dinner or a movie. To date, I've never attended a senior prom or even a formal school dance.

No matter what was going on in my personal life, I always maintained a sense of ambition in my professional life. After graduation from high school, I immediately enrolled in a program to earn my certification as a legal secretary. I would go on to complete the program and began interviewing for positions.

As with every new season, there is the manifestation of new life. Peter and I learned that a new life would make an entrance into ours. A new season was upon us. After four years of a budding romance and courtship, I learned that I was pregnant. Peter was ecstatic and it truly felt like life was unfolding as it should for us.

I had not completely determined how to break the news to my parents. I knew for certain that my mom would be upset. Strategy and a well-executed plan had always been my key to success when dealing with my parents. The first thing I did was go to the doctor to be certain that I was in fact pregnant. During the doctor's visit, I received an ultrasound, due date, and prenatal care, just in case my parents got angry enough to take me off of their insurance. During the ultrasound, I found out that I was having a girl. Peter was just as excited as I was. Now, I just had to find the right time to tell my parents.

I found the courage early one Saturday morning as my dad was getting ready to go sell items at the swap meet. My mother was in bed and I went into their room and broke the news to both of them at the same time.

"I have something to tell you," I said. I asked my father to take a seat and I told them that I was pregnant and showed them the ultrasound.

All my dad said was, "At least you waited until you graduated from high school."

My mom on the other hand was angry and had an unreasonable request. "You'd better not have a boy," she said.

As if there was a way that I could dictate the sex of the baby growing inside of me. My parents never questioned if Peter was the father or his position in my life because he had already been my boyfriend for four years. My dad left and I stayed to talk with my mother alone. During that time, I told her that I was having a girl and that I wanted her to name the baby. It seemed that another layer was revealed in my mother when it set in that I was having a girl and that she could truly determine her name. From that moment forward, my mom became obsessed with the prospect of new life. My daughter would be their first-born grandchild.

The initial reactions from our parents were as different as my interactions in both homes. Peter's parents were overjoyed and saw it as expansion of their family. The more the merrier was their mindset. They had all the space in the world in the country with the massive land that their home was positioned on. I would venture to say that his father believed that he could just keep adding on rooms to their existing home to make it big enough to accommodate any growth that their family witnessed. Although I knew that my parents were somewhat disappointed, they never once expressed that I would not still have their love and support, but I could tell that they had a different set of plans for how my life would unfold. The pregnancy also meant a new dynamic and layer for Peter and me. Wanting to ensure that we were taken care of, Peter rented an apartment for us and our growing family. Even though my parents did not allow me to move out and live with Peter on a full time basis, just knowing that he had gotten the apartment, proved to further cement our relationship and my trust for our future. I wanted to be with him and by this point believed that I had been lucky enough to discover true love much earlier than many of my counterparts whom I had attended school with.

Just when some aspects of life appear to come together, others unravel. I've heard it said that when one life arrives, another departs. As we continued making plans for the arrival of our baby, Peter learned that his mother was diagnosed with breast cancer. This was earth shattering for his entire family. She was the glue that bound everyone together, the rock, and source of strength — even mine. Everyone relied so heavily on her. In the midst of her sickness, the family took a noticeable nosedive. You could see the distance growing between the family members. The lively chatter that had once filled Peter's parent's bedroom evolved into deafening silence. Each of his brothers and sisters seemed to pick up their own agendas. Where it had once appeared that the family was on the same page, everyone now seemed to be ships in passing. Peter was no different. He too felt the lack of his mother's hands of guidance and wisdom. They were all desperately in need of her powerful prayers, but the truth is, she needed someone to pray for her and in my quiet moments, I did just that. Although she hadn't passed away, the family moved as if she did. I'm not sure if it would have helped Peter to stay at home rather than getting the apartment for us. Either way, he was losing his anchor.

One day, I was at Peter's apartment and glanced over as he sat at the kitchen table. I was lying on my side on the sofa in the adjoining living room. I continued to toss and turn because I couldn't seem to get comfortable as my stomach continued to grow. From the corner of my eye, I saw Peter leaning towards the table and moving his head up and down in a back and forth motion. I could hear him making a sniffing noise as if his nose was running. It was shocking to find him snorting cocaine. I truly didn't know what it was, but I instinctively knew that something wasn't right. I had never seen him do this before and I felt in my heart that much of his decision-making was based on hurt from his mother's sickness. Looking back, I believe that he was disoriented and maybe even feeling pressure about the arrival of our child. I wanted to get help for him. It pained me to see him in emotional distress and although his mother had not passed, she was no longer available in the ways in which she had previously been.

Over the years, I had developed a close relationship with his twin sisters, Chance and Chase. They were like my own sisters. Not knowing whom else I could turn to, I made the decision to call Chance and tell her what Peter was doing. My hope was that she could assist me in getting him the help that he needed, but to my surprise, she accused me of lying. It shook me and made me feel very insecure that she would believe that I would ever do anything to hurt Peter or the family. He was my family now too and we would all be connected forever through the birth of our child. I had always respected them so much and it crushed me to think that their opinion of me had changed so drastically.

The months of pregnancy continued to pass and the baby was healthy. Peter was still just as excited about our little girl as he had been in the beginning, and it was my hope that maybe the birth would be enough for him to shake the nasty drug habit that was now a part of who he was.

I continue working a job in the interim, as I interviewed for positions that would pay well for the certification that I had acquired. During the last week of my pregnancy,

I went to Toys R Us to pick up some more supplies for the baby. I was obsessed with making sure that we had all that we needed before she arrived. After leaving the store, I went to Peter's apartment and knocked on the door. There was no answer. I kept knocking until I got angry. For some reason, I believed that he was there and just not answering for me. Now men would have us believe that our intuition is off, but that's one of the many lies that men tell. A woman's intuition is never wrong. I became more aggressive in my knocking; resolved that come hell or high water I was getting in that apartment right then.

With pregnancy hormones raging, I busted through the window at the back of the apartment that led directly into the bedroom. I wasn't even sure how I was going to step through the window with my belly in tow, but at the time, I wasn't letting anything stop me. When I pulled back the curtain, it was as if my eyes were deceiving me. Peter was lying in the bed, butt ass naked, with another woman who I did not know. I lifted my leg and jumped through the window, landing on top of the TV stand. How in the world that thing didn't break is beyond me. Without thinking, I reached for a machete near the top of the wall that Peter had mounted as decoration and I dove towards the bed. In that moment of rage, I don't believe that I even remembered I was pregnant. The nerve of him!

Both Peter and the unidentified woman rose from the bed in fear and attempted to run towards the bathroom. I cornered them both off with the machete in my hand, tears in my eyes and rage in my soul. I began to hyperventilate. This was just too much to bear. "I can't catch my breath," I mumbled. I was leaning on the wall nearest to me as my body had given out.

"It's not what you think," said Peter.

"What the hell is it then? Huh? What the hell is going on?" I asked. I was discouraged and defeated.

Then, to add insult to injury, Peter kicked me while I was down. He looked me square in my eyes and said, "If you don't leave now, I'm going to call the police."

Instantly, the insanity that had taken up residence in my body, left. I turned around and walked towards the front door. I was far more calm than I was before I had arrived. I let myself out and drove home. When I arrived at my house, I told my mother about the events that had transpired.

"You don't have to do anything that you don't want to do and you are never alone," said my mother. In those moments, I knew that the love I often searched for was within the walls of the place that I had affectionately called home and even if it wasn't always the way that I wanted it to be, it was there and for that I was appreciative. I remained calm because I didn't want to harm our unborn daughter.

Later on that evening, Peter came by to apologize to me, but I was numb and all of my energy and attention had shifted to the baby growing inside of me. I had made up my mind that I was not going to allow him, or anyone else for that matter, destroy what God had created in me.

On July 28, 1990, the same day Roseanne Barr screwed up the National Anthem, I was admitted to Memorial Hospital in Bakersfield, California in preparation to give birth to my first child. Peter's whole family was present, all of his sisters and all of his brothers. My delivery was as normal as it could have been, although I had to have a C-section. Peter arrived late for the delivery. Apparently, he was at the nearby Elks Lodge telling folks that I was giving birth to his child.

I can honestly admit that I had my game face on. If he hadn't made it, I would have been disappointed, but not for the reasons that you might think. I wanted to give my daughter the life that she deserved, but my desire to be with Peter as we had once been, was diminished. I just couldn't wrap my mind around how he had changed in such a short period of time. Furthermore, deceit was not my cup of tea and I wasn't sure if I could trust him anymore. My happiness would now be rooted in something other than Peter.

After twenty hours of labor, and what felt like a lifetime to reflect, Talia Denise Larson was born. My mother had chosen the name after her favorite singer Talia Dayne.

She was the most beautiful person that I had ever seen. The doctors told us that she was healthy and I made up my mind right then and there that I was done with Peter. The minute that my baby was born, I became a single mom. This also meant that my level of ambition skyrocketed, as I believed Talia to be my responsibility. I wasn't sure how things would play out with Peter, but I was certain of my ability to provide a life for her.

All the interviews I had gone on while pregnant paid off. While in labor, I received a phone call offering me a position and in the middle of a contraction, I accepted. I was a fighter, not a quitter and now more than ever I needed a well-paying job. After the baby was born and the family began to settle down and clear out, Chance stayed back to speak with me privately and apologized for having accused me of lying about Peter's drug addiction. She admitted that she was scared and their family had been in such turmoil prior to the passing of her mother. I understood and accepted her apology. That night, as I lay in the hospital bed, I looked over at Talia, sleeping so peacefully in the portable, clear bin that hospitals used as cribs for newborn babies, and I promised her that she would never have to worry about being taken care of. I looked up at the ceiling, let out a deep sigh of relief, and uttered aloud the words, "New chapter."

4: CALIFORNIA DREAMIN'

"When people choose to walk away, you must ask yourself if they ever truly intended to stay."

Have you ever reached a crossroads in your life? What did you do? How did you determine your next move? I've been there as well and I've learned a thing or two about forks in the road. No matter what happens in life, you must learn to remain true to your intentions. There were many times that I wasn't sure of which direction to go in, but I was certain that remaining stagnant was not an option. I've always believed that life has more for me. I also knew that it was my responsibility to go and get it. Nothing would be given to me and that was OK. Even if you find yourself not knowing which way to move, never forget that backwards is not an option.

LIE #4: YOU GET WHAT YOU DESERVE.

I now lived full time at home with my parents. Everything about the house was the same, but everything about me was so different. I had left as a single teenage girl who'd found love, and I'd returned as a single mother, ready to carry the weight of the world on my shoulders. Even though I had not officially moved in with Peter and his family, or even with him in the apartment, I had spent so much time with Peter that it seemed I was never home. My mother and I began to encounter tremendous tension due to her obsession with Talia. Admittedly, my dad was enamored with the baby too, but my mother took it to an entirely different level. She would wake up in the middle of the night to feed her, she redecorated my entire room in all white eyelet, even the crib and when we went out, she had to be the one holding the baby My mom's controlling ways often brought out the worst in me. One day, the tension mounted so high that in the midst of a heated exchange I told her, "Go have your own baby!" It was all I could say to keep from swearing and being any further disrespectful.

As a new mom, you are already in a space of uneasiness because it's all so new. I only wanted to be the best mother that I could for Talia, but nothing I did was good enough for my mother. I had my own feelings about everything and I felt like no one took this into consideration. I was so torn. I wanted to be independent, but I was really still very hurt. I loved Peter. I was happy to have had his daughter even though he now had a flourishing drug problem and acted a damn fool consistently. His beloved mother had now passed and life for him and the entire family was different.

I wasn't quite sure if life at home with my new baby was what would make me happy. My heart was still broken and in desperate need of repair or at least something or someone to take my mind off of all that had happened. Even though I loved Peter, my willingness to be with him and work to regain the trust that had been so brutally destroyed, was not an option. My heart seemed to close itself off from the person that was the source of its pain. Although broken and bruised, my ability to love never left. I lived and breathed for the prospect of love. Many would have given up after experiencing the type of pain that Peter caused me, but I wasn't a quitter. Some say love is a losing game, but I have always been willing to try.

Even as a new mom, I tried to live my life. I received a call from my friend Inglesia, inviting me to meet her at a local restaurant. I was looking forward to catching up with her. As I walked toward the restaurant, I must have been looking at my feet because I didn't notice that someone was holding the door open for me. Still looking down, I felt the warmth of a hand on mine and noticed a pair of really nice looking men's tennis shoes; brand new, white, Air Force Ones, were all the rage at the time. As I looked up, I saw the owner of the shoes. It was him! I almost peed my pants, but thankfully my body was frozen and that included my bladder. It was like an out of body experience.

"Are you gonna just keep standing there?" he asked.

I couldn't speak and when I finally managed to open my mouth, I realized it was a mistake. All that came out was, "Uuh, yeah. I mean. . .Yes. I mean. . . No. I mean . . . thank you. Yes! Thank you for holding the door." Good lord, I was literally shaking.

"I've been watching you for a while. You should let me call you sometime," he said. He was so damn smooth. I think I felt faint. Then he handed me a pen and the receipt from his meal. "Just write your number right here." I could barely control my hands, but I managed to scribble my number down and he said, "Alright. Talk soon."

My mouth had lost the ability to form words and considering how eloquent I had already been, it was probably for the best. I stood there in silence, staring after him. Desmond had just asked me for my number.

What can be said of Desmond? I haven't mentioned him until now because there was really nothing to say. The fact was that I had a crush on him that was indescribable, but nothing had ever come of it. I was too nervous around him to have ever acted on any impulses and furthermore, Peter had always been my guy and I wouldn't have done anything to disrespect our relationship. Desmond remained just a distant dream; someone I admired from afar.

He and I had attended the same high school and from the moment I laid eyes on him, I was slightly infatuated. He was statuesque and a little lanky, but he stood with this arch in his back and I imagined him hugging me, his body curving towards mine. He had this jerry curl that was long and so sexy to me. His clothes were always well put together and it was obvious that he took the time to iron everything with pride. He was meticulous right down to his tennis shoes. In high school, I would pass him every day as he stood under the Nigga Tree when I was walking to class. He just stood out, even in the crowd. At least to me he did. Desmond looked like the perfect gentleman in a school full of horny high school boys. Moreover, it wasn't just his looks; he had the best personality in the world. Never in my entire life had anyone made me feel warm on the inside at just the thought of them. There was just something about him. All of these things and more explain why I just couldn't manage to gain my composure at the restaurant. I would never know if he knew how I had felt about him all this time, but I would soon find out.

Desmond began calling me regularly. At the time, he lived with his grandfather. We clicked almost instantly. The personality that I had admired so much was now a part of my everyday laughter and happiness. Desmond was caring and kind and showed such a gentle side, even with Talia. He would often hold her and give her a bottle while I cooked dinner for him and his grandfather. We truly enjoyed the simple things and most of all spending quality time together. We traveled to nearby beaches, and went on dinner dates nonstop. It was a whirlwind romance, but I truly enjoyed being in his presence. I felt like I could just be myself and he accepted me for who I was. I had always wondered if I would ever be able to find love again as a single parent, but he never judged me. As the days past, I grew to admire him more and more.

He was one of the few people that had I met that truly had a blueprint for what he wanted to manifest in his life. He had gone to school to become an educator and that is exactly what he did. I was impressed with his determination to follow his dreams. I found it sexy that he spent his days as an elementary school teacher, grooming the future generations for success. It turned me on when I imagined him at work. He was so predictable sometimes. He sat at in the same desk like clockwork to grade his students' papers. Sometimes, I would make surprise visits after the students were dismissed. I'd position myself at his feet under the desk and give him head. I'm not sure who was more turned on, him or me. I just knew that seeing him in his tie and dress pants, neatly creased and his button up shirt drove me crazy. I guess I saw myself having a future with him. I felt in my heart that Desmond, Talia, and I could be a family.

The passion between us continued to grow and another life was conceived. When I discovered that I was pregnant for the second time, now with Desmond's baby, I was distraught. I knew that I wasn't ready for another child. Talia was only six months old. I was still living with my mother and father and the thought of being a mother of two was too much for me to bear. In my heart, I also felt like having a baby would be an undeniable distraction for Desmond. He had been so diligent in his career and he was making amazing progress towards his new goal of becoming an administrator. I truly had his best interest at heart. After a heart to heart, we mutually agreed that neither of us was ready to accept responsibility for another life. I made the decision to terminate the pregnancy. It was truly my decision. It scared me emotionally because I had witnessed the beauty of new life and I wanted nothing more than to build a life with Desmond. The timing was just not right. After the abortion, our relationship began to dwindle. The multiple conversations each day turned into once a day and eventually, we both stopped calling. We just stopped falling in love. There were no hard feeling and no love was lost, we just seemed to have lost each other.

I began focusing more on my career goals and determining what my next steps would be. One afternoon, I returned home from work and I had just taken Talia out of her baby seat when the phone rang. It was Inglesia.

"Did you know that Desmond was dating Ally?" she said.

"What do you mean?" I asked.

"I know it may sound crazy, but I found out that Desmond has been dating Ally the entire time that you guys were together. I saw them together."

My heart dropped. Could this have been why he just let me slip out of his grasp? Was he with her when I was pregnant? Now it all began to make sense to me. I was enraged. I had been civil about our parting but I wasn't so sure that I would have managed to be so, had I known that there was someone else involved. I knew exactly who Ally was. To make matters worse, she worked at the same hospital that my mother worked at. I turned into an investigator instantly. I was determined to get to the bottom of it that night. In the midst of my search, I somehow discovered her phone number. With tears in my eyes, I dialed the numbers on the phone so hard that my finger slipped off of one of the buttons. I still managed to call the correct number.

"Hello," a soft voice answered the phone.

A tear fell from my eye, as I forced myself to gain what was left of my composure. "Is this Ally? I just want to let you know, I just had an abortion by your man." I slammed the phone down as hard as I could. In that moment, I hoped that she felt some part of the pain that I felt. I didn't wish her any ill because I know that it wasn't her fault, but I had nowhere else to place my disdain for the deceit.

Even after all of that, Desmond never called. He never asked me why I had contacted her. He never called me to try to make things right. To add insult to injury, I later learned that they got married. He chose her and not me.

I was forced to close another chapter of life and love. I guess everything happens for a reason. My mother and father were suffocating me in their attempts to care for Talia. While their kindness was appreciated, I needed to sort things out and find a way to spread my wings. If I stayed in Bakersfield, there was a good chance that I would lose myself. I was desperate for a change. On a Monday, I received a call that a job that I had previously applied for in Sacramento wanted to make an offer. By that Friday, I had managed to pack all of Talia and my belongings and we were on the road to begin a new life. No more Peter, no more Desmond, and no more heartache.

5: A DIFFERENT POINT OF VIEW

"Love is a gift. You must unwrap it when it is present."

I am sure that by now, you are having mixed feelings about me, but keep reading, there's more. The real truth is that I'm no different from any other human being who wants to be loved. Some search an entire lifetime for it. I'm one of those people, but I know it when I see it, even if it doesn't withstand the test of time. Love must be felt when it is present and I pity the people who can't recognize it. I'm not saying that you should take whatever someone throws your way, but I am saying that we get so stuck on finding the perfect person that we miss the opportunities to just experience life and love. I left myself open and never gave up on love, even though there was the probability of more heartbreak in my future. I figured, maybe, just maybe, love would love me back.

LIE #5: I'M NOT LOOKING FOR MY MOTHER.

After moving to Sacramento, my mindset was different. I was no longer a little girl looking for love. I was a woman and admittedly, I had needs. My needs were not my driving force or my motivation, but I never fell short in that department. Not only was I in search of a man to satisfy me, but also to make a positive difference in my life. I was never really concerned about Talia being take care of because I knew that come hell, or high water, I would ensure it. I just wondered if there would ever be anyone who would take care of my heart. I didn't harbor any resentment for all of the things that had happened in the past, and I resolved to let the past be the past. I felt like a fresh start was just what I needed to turn over a new leaf.

I began working a government job at Folsom State Prison. The prison was newly opened and there were many procedures that the staff had to go through in order to receive the proper clearances. I worked in the infirmary and one of the clearance activities was a check of each employee's driver's license. When they ran my driver's license, it was determined that my license was suspended. I was afraid that I would lose my job. While there, a Sergeant, who was at least fifteen years my senior, called me into his office and he officially told me that my license was suspended. I was so nervous. I needed to maintain my employment to care of Talia. "Don't worry about it. We will take care of it," he said. From that day forward, he took an interest in me.

As I was driving into work one day, I became stranded due to a flat tire. I felt hopeless, as I had no one to call. Eventually, I remembered that I had the Sergeant's business card in the back pocket of my uniform pants. I was hesitant as I stared at the number on the card. I did not want to compromise my professional relationship with him, but I had no one else. I dialed his number and to my surprise, he answered on the first ring. I explained in desperation that I was stranded and asked him if there was any way that he could help me make it into work? There was a brief pause and I held my breath, waiting for him to deny my request.

"I'll be right there, just stay where you are," he said.

When he arrived, he suggested exchanged cars with me and asked if I would be comfortable driving his car back to the facility. "Hell yeah," I thought to myself. I would have never said that out loud, but I could hardly contain my excitement. He had a brand new BMW and I most certainly had not driven or even been in one before. We exchanged keys and I drove myself to work. When I arrived, I sat for a while in the parking lot and thought to myself how the Sergeant had saved me. About two hours later, he called the phone at my desk and asked me to meet him in the parking lot to exchange keys. As I approached the front door of the facility, I saw that he had parked my car out front and he was standing next to it as if he were proud. I walked down the sidewalk and made my way over to him. It was then that I noticed that my car had been detailed and the tire was fixed.

"Here you are little lady. It's as good as new," he said.

"Are those new tires?" I asked, shocked.

He nodded with a crooked grin.

"You put new tires on the whole car?"

The Sergeant again shook his head in confirmation.

"Sir, I can't afford that. I am not even sure when I would be able to pay you back for all of this."

"Just say that you'll have dinner with me," he replied.

It became apparent that he was pursuing me, which was why he helped me in the first place. I returned the smile and nodded my head. I was willing to try my hand at love and in this case, it would prove to be lust. We began going out to dinner regularly. We also began sleeping together. Initially, I was worried that things would be weird at work, but because of his position, we didn't see each other often. On some occasions, he would sneak into my office and close the blinds and we would have quickies on my lunch break.

It was different being with someone who was fifteen years my senior, but he was the option on the table. After about a month of dating him, I began to distance myself because he often had requests during intimacy that I was not accustomed to, and they made me feel uncomfortable. Neither Peter nor Desmond had ever really requested any fetish type needs from me. The Sergeant, however, was different. I remember during one particular evening he wanted me to say, "I'm daddy's bitch." Had he lost his mind? First of all, he wasn't my daddy, and second of all, I was nobody's bitch. Right in the middle of being intimate with him, I got up, got dressed, and left. I vowed to never engage with him again. That wasn't my cup of tea and it felt like the beginning of some superiority crap. I wanted nothing further to do with him. I should have known something was wrong with him when I learned that he had a daughter that was very close in age to me. What man wants to date a woman who could be his daughter? I ran as fast as I could to an entirely different city.

I withdrew money from my savings, packed our belongings, and drove with haste to Sacramento. We moved in with my cousin Tracy, just until I could get my bearings and get established. I knew that driving that old car would be risky, but I attempted anyway. I needed a change of scenery. That car has brought me nothing but bad luck. I mean, look how it led me to the Sergeant. Thankfully, we made it to Sacramento on a wing and a prayer, but the car needed a funeral upon arrival. Tracy was kind enough to take me to work and pick me up until I could figure something else out. I'll never forget that she was driving an old Z28. Sacramento was calm. There was no one there hovering over me and telling me how to take care of my baby. There were also no remnants of the men and my past, which I left behind.

I can recall a Wednesday afternoon that Tracy wanted a break from the monotony. She turned up the music in the car and rolled down the windows. The sun was beaming through the windshield and it kissed her hands. It was a beautiful day in Sacramento and I closed my eyes to feel the breeze.

"I'm going to stop by a friend's house before we pick Talia up from school today, Cousin," she exclaimed. She always called me Cousin. It was a term of endearment.

"Who's house?" I inquired.

"Frank's. They are over there having a good old time."

I could hear the excitement in her voice. I had no desire to go, but I also couldn't bring myself to spoil her fun, as she had been so kind to me. Tracy spoke of Frank often and all I knew was that he was one of her smoking partners. They smoked weed and laughed together on many occasions. It was the thing to do. As we pulled up to the house, I was more reserved than usual.

"You go on in. I'll stay here in the car," I said.

"Girl! No way in hell I'm leaving you here," Tracy answered.

"No way in hell I'm goin in." She knew that I was serious and when I put my foot down it meant the end of the discussion.

I could see that the door was open and I could hear the voices. Were these fools having a house party in the middle of the week? Whatever, it had absolutely nothing to do with me. Tracy hopped out of the car and rolled her eyes at me sarcastically. She then began to switch a little, she looked over her shoulder, and we laughed. She was cute and she knew it.

After about ten minutes of sitting there, I got a little warm. I cranked the handle to roll down the window further. I was facing down toward the handle of the window when I heard a voice. It sounded close to me.

"Hey. Say . . . why didn't you come in? Everyone is in there having a good time. Why are you out here?" he asked.

As I looked up, I noticed a statuesque man, who was now blocking the sun. He just kept talking to me as if he knew that I was paying attention. I squinted a bit to see him in detail. He was big like a quarterback. I couldn't tell if he played football or if he was just a big guy. He had broad shoulders and a very wide back. His head was freshly shaven and he was bald. As he talked, I noticed the gaps between each of his teeth. He kind of reminded me of Charles Barkley, the NBA player. As a matter of fact, they could have been brothers.

"I'm Ryan by the way. Ryan Suarez." He extended his hand just above the glass and I extended mine. As we shook hands, he began asking a series of questions that almost felt like an interrogation, but I could tell that someone had already told him a few things about me. That had to have been Tracy because I didn't know anyone else. I had just moved to Sacramento.

"So, who are you dating?" he asked.

I lied and told him that I was dating Desmond. I even went so far as to describe him, though I'm not sure why. Maybe I was trying to let him know that he wasn't my type.

I can't say that I was prepared for his response but he said, "When you get tired of dating them jerry curl ass niggas, give me a call." He wrote his number on a small sheet of paper and handed it to me. He held my hand for a little longer after giving me the paper. Shortly after our exchange, Tracy came out and hopped in the car. She smiled in a sly way as if she knew what was going on. She waved goodbye to Ryan and so did I and we departed to pick up the baby.

"It's not what you think, Cousin. I am here to get myself in order. I don't have time to be thinking of anyone else right now," I exclaimed.

"Mmhmm," Tracy murmured and smiled.

Thankfully, that was the end of that conversation and good riddance to Ryan. Now, if you believe that last sentence you might be just as much a romantic fool as me.

After being in Sacramento for a few months, I found myself longing for companionship. I just needed a friend or someone to talk to. Tracy had a life of her own and we had infringed on each other enough. As I sat peering out of my bedroom window, I noticed the piece of paper that Ryan had written his number on. It was crumbled, as I had assured myself that I would never use it, but curiosity got the better of me. I just had to see what, if anything, would come of it. It was an innocent phone call right? I walked over to the dresser and reached for the wrinkled paper. As I unfolded it, my mind wandered to my past relationships and how they had affected who I was. Would this turn out to be another ship that would sail in and out of my life? Well, that wouldn't happen if I only remained friends with him. I kept telling myself that as I dialed Ryan's number. I almost hated that I had a desire to call him.

"Hello?" he answered on the first ring.

"H. . hell. . .hello," I stuttered. "Is Ryan available please?" I could hardly get my words together.

"I've been waiting for you to call," he said in a throaty voice.

I can honestly say that after the first conversation, I knew that he could be my friend. He wasn't my type and I did not have love on the brain, but I knew that developing a friendship with him was exactly what I wanted to do. I learned more about him as the days passed and the more we talked on the phone. Ryan, like me, was employed by the Department of Corrections, and unlike anyone I had ever dated. He did not like to engage in any form of conflict and followed a minimalist lifestyle. These attributes were attractive to me because I think that simplicity was exactly what I needed in my life at that time. I had watched my mother covet the finer things in life, and I had followed in her footsteps. Ryan on the other hand had never even heard of stores like Neiman Marcus or Macy's. I liked the fact that he saw no need to compete with others for material things. He just didn't see the value in them. When we would visit other people's homes, his personal preferences became evident. He'd make comments like, "Oh my God, you live in a mansion?" or "Are you guys rich?" I'll admit, this behavior was a turnoff, but he was simple and that was cool with me.

As I dug deeper to discover more, I learned that many of his relationships with his family members were strained. He didn't have a relationship with his mother and he was not very close to his brother. His backstory made me compassionate towards him. His mother was just eleven years old when she became pregnant with him and being of Mexican descent, her parents disapproved of her carrying a black man's child. As a result, they sent her to have an abortion. She couldn't bring herself to go through with it, so she continued to carry the baby until she was full term. Just as she gave birth, her parents encouraged her to erase all remnants of the black man that she had engaged with, by putting her baby boy up for adoption. Reluctantly, she completed the paperwork and never saw her newborn baby in the hospital. About a week after his birth and signing the paperwork, she received a call from the agency telling her that she had signed on the wrong line. When she went back correct the papers, she caught a glimpse of the son that she had never held and could not bear the thought of giving him away to another family. She kept him and named him Ryan.

As her life unfolded, she discovered that she was pregnant by another black man. She was a single mother with two sons, which meant two mouths to feed. She began selling drugs to support her family. She was a hard worker. In her parents' eyes, she was unfit and reckless. Her selling drugs was the exact opposite of what Ryan's grandfather had taught her. He looked down upon her. Nevertheless, she was the kind of woman that would do whatever it took to make a life for her children. Even though her work was illegal, her work ethic was never questioned.

By the time I met her, she had given her life to God and her passion, drive, and determination was to lead a life that she could be proud of and one that reflected a pious being.

If I was going to be close to Ryan, it was important for me to find out more about his mom. I dug deeper and sought to establish a connection with her, even though he did not have one. After learning of her story, I empathized with her. I knew that she understood the struggle of being a single mom, but she had been just a kid having babies by black men. I finally convinced

Ryan to take me to meet her. We visited her church, as that is where she spent most of her time.

She was of the apostolic religion and when I met her, there was an automatic connection. I knew that it would be meaningful if I could connect Ryan more deeply with her. His heart was broken from all that had unfolded in his mother's past and knowing that she had been planning to put him up for adoption. It's amazing what stays deeply rooted in your soul. Even though she went back for him and was moved not to leave him there after seeing him, there was always a part of him that believed that he was unwanted. My growing relationship with her, brought Ryan closer to her as well. I became the glue that bound them together. We began attending her church in Merced regularly. From the moment I met her, she was such a sweet lady and I could tell that Ryan's heart was less hardened towards her.

I'd grown to want more than a friendship with Ryan. I wanted a relationship with him, and I wanted him to want the same with me. He said he wanted the same, but his actions didn't always prove it. Aside from his mother, Ryan was always reluctant to take me around any of his other family members. He would never take me home to meet his grandparents. I felt inside that he was ashamed of the fact that I was black.

Understanding the circumstances of someone's story is so important. It brings light to so many of their mannerisms and the ways in which they perceive the world.

The truth is that Ryan was raised by a Mexican family, who did not view blacks favorably. I don't think he ever could or did understand black people. And even though we both had melanin imbedded in our skin, there were times that I felt like he just didn't get me. It still amazes me that you can have so much in common with a person and at the same time, nothing at all. The things that we did have in common were enough for me to continue spending time with him. I eventually became Ryan's girlfriend, though he never formally claimed me as such. I operated in that space and saw myself making changes to be with him — to be more like the women of his ethnicity. My hope was that he would accept me. Deep down inside, I also wanted to accept myself.

As I continued to work for the state, in a different sector of the Department of Corrections, I never stopped doing what was best for Talia and me. I had a supervisor named Barbara Easton, or Barb for short, who simply hated me and I wasn't sure how long I would last in the position I held. I never understood her dislike of me. I came to work every day and did exactly what I was asked to do, but she always seemed to have it out for me. Maybe she was just miserable in her role and wanted to make life intolerable for others. She had to have been at least 110 years old. Her skin was leathery and I don't believe that any kind of facial could have made a difference for her. She smoked cigarettes and it looked like they had dried out all of the nourishment from her face. At the time, I smoked cigarettes too and she was my continuous motivation to quit the habit. I didn't want to look like her. She had this tacky pink lipstick that she would wear and it made a ring around her cigarette. Her hair was mud brown with the finest curls that I had ever seen and so thin that you could see her scalp with a simple glance. She wore an olive green uniform and the bottom hem of her pants would hover over the rim of the ugliest black tennis shoes with huge rubber soles. Sometimes, if I looked hard enough,I could see a hint of her white socks peeking out. She was a hot mess. Regardless of all of that, her confidence level must have been diminished because she'd been released from a supervisor position in another department for misappropriation of funds. Don't ask me how she finagled another supervisor position. However she managed it, her attitude towards me never improved. Maybe she was mean because she was released from her former position. Maybe she was mad because she didn't really want to be there. Maybe, she just hated my guts. Whatever the reason, she was a wreck and she hated my guts. Believe me when I say that the feeling was mutual. She made my life hell, such to the point that I wasn't sure of how much more I could take. From the constant threats to write me up, to the way she rolled her eyes at me daily when walking by my desk, I was not having fun.

It seemed that the more simple things became, the more complicated life felt. I was still staying with Tracy and found myself frustrated that I hadn't gotten on my feet as quickly as I had anticipated. Moreover, I had never really dealt with the hurt that Peter and Desmond had caused. To top things off, the fact that Ryan hadn't taken the initiative to make a definite commitment to me, made me feel insecure. Who wouldn't feel that way?

I began having terrible headaches again and on a Monday, I remember waking up and declaring that I needed a vacation. One thing that I never did was miss work, and I hadn't up until this point. I booked a rental car and a hotel in Las Vegas. It was still on the west coast, but far enough that I could just get away and clear my mind. I put in a request that day at work with the supervisor who was Barb's boss. I knew that if I had told Barb that I needed to take a stress week, she would have found a way to write me up for it. When I got back to Tracy's apartment, I asked her if she would be willing to keep Talia for me and she agreed. I picked up the phone and immediately called Ryan.

"Hello," he said.

"Let's go to Vegas for a while."

Softly he said, "OK."

That was all I needed to hear.

The next morning, Ryan helped me pick up the rental car and off into the morning sunrise we drove. Six hours later when we got to the hotel room, the light was blinking on the phone. How could anyone have known that I was there? I thought that maybe the hotel had created a welcome message of some sort. I picked up the phone and listened intently. It was a message from Barb's boss, the same one who had granted me permission to take the leave.

"Hello, Rachel. When you get back from your trip, I would like to see you in my office."

That message was the start of a ripple effect of negativity. The trip was an overall disaster. Ryan didn't want to walk the strip. He didn't want to do anything. I began questioning why he had agreed to come. It was an utter waste of time. Not to mention, I now had that strange message hanging over my head. I couldn't wait to get back home to Talia. She was the only person that I missed. She was really all that I had.

When I returned to work, I walked in, placed my bag down in the usual spot, and turned on my computer to begin checking status reports. As I sat, I noticed a little brown thing moving on my desk. I bent in to get a closer look and jumped up in haste while screaming in terror. It was a scorpion. I knew exactly who had put it there. That bitch, Barbara was trying to kill me. I knew that she put it there because she lived in the mountains near Lake Tahoe and scorpions were known to live there. Right then, in that moment, I knew that I could never return to that desk or that job again. I never reported it or told the union. There was no way to prove she had put it there.

So there I was, on my third relationship that appeared to be traveling to destination nowhere, with a man whom I had grown to adore that had no intention of staking any claim to me. I couldn't just stick around and waste all of my good years with him with the prospect of no commitment. To add insult to injury, I was trapped in a job that I hated, with a prehistoric supervisor out for my blood. When I placed all of my chips on the table, I was forced to acknowledge that there was not one thing holding me in Sacramento, except what I felt to be a bed of lies. Lies that Ryan's actions would turn into real love, lies that Barb would somehow manage to fall off the face of the earth, and lies that I would be able to make financial gains much faster in order to support Talia and myself. I had had enough.

After a long hard look in the mirror, I made up my mind. I didn't even bother reporting to work the next day. Instead, I spent the morning typing my resignation letter. I made a call to withdraw what was left of my retirement, all $19,000, which would be enough for a fresh start. I had one agenda in mind — packing.

Sometimes you win and sometimes you lose, but either way, you learn. Why is it that the most valuable lessons have to hurt so much? If I could teach the world anything, it would be that you can't allow your heart to harden because things don't go as planned. Life is as much about the journey as it is the destination. As they say, a calm sea does not qualify a skillful sailor.

6: THE PIECES OF ME

*"If anyone ever treats you like you are ordinary,
disregard them."*

For every ending, there is a new beginning. New beginnings for me signified two things, the opportunity to pick up the pieces of myself that had been scattered, and the potential for prosperity. There was a glimmer of hope for what could be, and it proved to be a more powerful force than ever imagined. Maybe everyone feels the same way, but I knew that I was special. Did anyone else recognize it? As I said, there's always hope.

LIE #6: I AM READY FOR LOVE.

I found myself standing in the middle of a parking lot filled with cars and I decided that one of them would be mine. There was no way that I was going to hitch hike a ride to our next destination. I had driven Talia and myself to Sacramento and I sure as hell planned to drive us away. I picked a silver, four-door Toyota. It had just enough space for us and it had a shine that wasn't showy, but classy. It was me all the way. I paid cash for it from the money that I had deducted from my savings and drove off the lot with the car paid and full. When I returned to Tracy's, all I had to do was put our belongings in the car. As I pulled up, she was standing at the front window holding Talia. I could tell that she didn't agree with my leaving. She began talking before I could even open the door.

"You know you don't have to do this right? You know that you guys are more than welcome to stay here with me?"

I could tell that it upset her to see us go, but she understood that I needed to do what was best for Talia and me. After getting everything packed into the car, it was pretty much full. I was careful to leave space to ensure that Talia would be safe and sound in the backseat.

I had received a new map from the dealership, but I knew where we were headed next. I had traveled the route many times on family trips when I was a little girl. Talia and I hit the road for a very short drive and when I saw the sign that said Oakland, sixty-two miles, I knew that I had made the right decision. Growing up, we would visit Oakland multiple times a year to spend time with my aunt Mattie who lived there. As we drove through the neighborhood, I remember thinking that there was so much I hadn't noticed as a little girl. It was a little rough. My aunt had told us the ongoing stories of people getting gunned down amidst gang violence. I'm sure my senses were heightened because I had more to think about than just myself. I continued to drive through town and I began to see a pattern. On each street corner stood the fellas in the white t-shirts and jeans, and behind them was either a liquor store or a church. I guess in life, we have to choose which spirit we allow to take precedence.

Aunt Mattie had been in Oakland all of her life and she showed no signs of being frightened of any of it. As we got closer to her house, I could see that she was standing on her front porch waiting for us. Our family was always hospitable in that way.

"Bring me that baby," she said, as she walked over to the car. She looked good. She was a particularly short lady who never really seemed to age. She had the same long, beautiful hair that my mother did and the ends of her ponytail were curly like ringlets. Her hair was salt and pepper and her caramel skin was silky. She wore very little makeup and she didn't need it. She always wore these pearl earrings that had a little diamond at the bottom. They appeared to be two different earrings but they were not. Simple hints like that were indicators to me that she liked the finer things in life.

As we walked into her home, I noticed the burglar bars on all of the windows and the front door. Aunt Mattie kept a key in the door and it was second nature for her to lock the door behind us. She left the door open to allow the fresh air in and the daunting heat from the Oakland sun to escape. At no point were we not secure in her home.

After having been there for about an hour, the doorbell rang. To my surprise, it was both of my sisters. They too had moved to Oakland. We sat for hours with Aunt Mattie in the kitchen catching up. It had been a few months since they last saw Talia and we had an amazing time. We reminisced over the old memories that we had created together. Some good and some I wanted to forget, but what I couldn't deny was that there was a genuine love that we all shared for each other. I felt that there was potential for me to develop even more of a relationship with my sisters. The years between us didn't seem to matter as much.

It was a Sunday and we agreed that we needed to end the night, but we swore that we wouldn't let it be long before we enjoyed each other like this again. I kissed both of my sisters on the cheek and waved them goodbye from the porch.

"Let's get you guys inside. It's dark out here," said Aunt Mattie. I knew what she really meant. She had every intention of keeping us safe from the Oakland streets. I was too tired to unpack, but my heart was full. That night, I lay in the bed that Aunt Mattie had dressed in beautiful pink linens for us and I could see a little of the sky from the bedroom window. Maybe I was too tired and I imagined it, but I swore that I saw a shooting star. Whatever it was, I remember feeling that everything was going to be OK.

The next morning, I woke up, showered, and proceeded to pull my black pencil skirt and white button up shirt with the collar from my luggage. The shirt was so wrinkled; there was no way that I could get away with not ironing it. I didn't have much time and ironing was not part of the agenda, but nevertheless, it had to be done. The frenzy of dressing and leaving the house continued from there. For the life of me, I could not find my other black pump and there was no way that I was wearing panty hose in that heat. I hopped from the house to the car and discovered that I had left the other heel in the car on the floor of the backseat. Maybe it had fallen out of one of the bags during the travel. I didn't care; I just needed to get to the interview on time. It had been lined up for over a two weeks. The same morning that I typed my resignation letter, I had also spent time searching for jobs in Oakland.

After hobbling out of the door, Aunt Mattie met me there with Talia in her hands. "Good luck baby. You can do it," she said. Talia didn't even cry. She was always so intuitive. I could tell by the look in her eyes. Even though she was too young to verbalize it, she knew that I was trying to make a better life for us.

It took me a solid twenty minutes to find my way. I was a little nervous, as this job would be in a field that I hadn't yet worked in. Waters Property Management, the sign read as I pulled into the parking lot. The office building was nice and it was obvious that this company had been doing well. It was chic. I parked my car and put my heels back on, as I had thrown them in the back and driven barefoot to the office. Walking up to the building, I had a good feeling. I guess anything would have been better than continuing to bear witness to Barb's ancient ass — anything.

I was greeted at the receptionist desk by a younger gentleman who appeared to be about eighteen or so. He was suited and booted, everyone in the office was. As I sat in the lobby waiting to be called for the interview, I noticed everyone that passed by said, "Hello". I could tell that the culture of the company was a positive one. It really seemed like a place that I would not mind being a part of.

"Rachel Larson, Ms. Waters will see you now."

"Thank you," I said and smiled. I was escorted down a long hallway with ivory-coated walls and expensive paintings sparsely scattered. I'm sure they were replicas, but whoever was in charge of the decor had impeccable taste.

"Ms. Waters, this is Rachel Larson," said the receptionist.

"Please have a seat. Thank you for coming today," she said softly. Ms. Waters looked like she could have been my age or even a little younger. She was dressed in a white suite that appeared to be St. John. I had seen suits like that in one of those expensive mailings that my mother always spent so much time perusing. I knew quality when I saw it. Under the St. John suit, she wore a white blouse that appeared to be silk. Her outfit was on point. I smiled when I saw her because there was a familiarity that I could identify with. After she returned to her seat, she sat down slowly as she glanced at me. There was a moment of silence as I prepared for the first round of questions. Five minutes into the interview, we were off topic.

"Have you had a chance to see the movie, 'Waiting to Exhale'?" I could tell that she was in need of someone to share her sentiments with. I can't quite remember what hit the conversation off, but what I do know is that the interview morphed into a conversation had by girlfriends. I heard footsteps coming down the hallway and the receptionist popped his head into the office.

"Ms. Waters, your eleven o'clock has arrived." I knew that meant that it was time for me to depart, but I must admit, I enjoyed it. I hadn't laughed like that with a girlfriend in quite some time. Even if I didn't get the job, I enjoyed the exchange.

I stopped to pick up lunch for myself, Talia, and my aunt. I arrived back at her home around one o'clock. Just as I walked in the door, the phone rang.

"Can you get that baby?" said Aunt Mattie.

I grabbed the receiver. "Hello?"

"May I speak with Rachel Larson please?"

"This is she."

Before I could finish, I heard the voice say, "You've got the job, Girl. This will be a no brainer for you," she said. "Do you have any questions for me?"

"I sure do. When do I start?"

After a mandatory four day training, I began working in the new role the following Monday. I knew that I needed to go out and get some more clothes for work. I needed to step my game up to work out of that office. It was the first time that I had really done anything for myself in quite some time. Working for the state, meant wearing the uniforms that were provided. Prior to that time, I had not had to concern myself with looking good for work.

On my first day, I woke up early to dress myself and get Talia ready to stay with my aunt. It took me even more time to find a full time babysitter that I felt comfortable leaving her with, but I knew that for now she was in good hands with Aunt Mattie.

As I drove up to the building, I had the same positive feelings that I felt the day that I interviewed. I just felt like something good was in store for me. I needed it now more than ever. My first day went off without a hitch and it felt like the rest would be history.

As Ms. Waters mentioned, it was a no brainer for me. I had the personality to keep the job light and upbeat. The job pretty much required me to be exactly who I was and to assist people in finding a rental property that met their needs. Half the battle was looking the part.

After a few months of working in the new position, I felt like I was settling into a life in Oakland. One of my colleagues at work also had a young daughter who attended a home daycare just down the street from my Aunt Mattie's house and I enrolled Talia there. I even started going to a hair salon regularly that was not too far from my job to get new haircuts. Taking pride in my appearance proved to be a self-esteem booster for me and I needed it. Dare I say it, but life was good.

The seasons changed and so did my desire to be in love. I was falling in love with the idea of caring for myself and for Talia. My next move was to find an apartment of our own.

One evening, while driving home from a quick run to the store, I was at a stoplight when I noticed a man in a car in the next lane looking at me. I did a double take because I wasn't sure if he was signaling for directions. The street was very busy as people were headed out, dressed in costumes to celebrate Halloween. I had no idea that adults took Halloween so seriously, but I guess for the majority of my life, I had been hiding under a rock. I had never actually been to a Halloween party.

"You should smile," he yelled from his car.

I allowed myself to gaze for a moment. He had one of the most beautiful smiles that I had ever seen. He was charming from afar. I laughed innocently. I guess I hadn't smiled from any words that a man had spoken in quite some time.

"What's your name beautiful?"

"Rachel," I whispered. I guess I was talking way too low.

"I'm sorry, what did you say?"

The noise from the people around us was loud. He motioned for me to pull over to a well-lit gas station just down the street. I had my daughter in the car, which made me think twice, but I knew that we were in the presence of several witnesses. My curiosity led me to want to hear what this man had to say. As I pulled over, he parked his car and walked over to mine. I sat with a girlish grin on my face as he walked over. It looked as if he was walking in slow motion. He skin was like caramel. He was clean-shaven and had a small triangle of hair just under his bottom lip. It was sexy as hell. He had to have been about six foot two and he walked with a little gap in his legs. As he got closer, I could see in more detail his features. He had very full eyebrows that perfectly framed his almond brown eyes. His pupils were so dark that they looked like black marbles. His eyelashes were full and long. He had on a pair of black jeans and a light blue, long sleeve, button down shirt, and the bottom button was left undone. I could see a hint of chest hair playing peek a boo at the top of his chest from the buttons up top left undone. The wind blew it open as he walked over.

"Is that your daughter in the back?" he inquired. His face lit up as if to imply that she was beautiful. Of course she was. I knew that for myself. "I want to give you my number. You were too gorgeous sitting there at the light for me not to take a chance on asking you if we could connect. Would you mind giving me yours?" he persisted.

"When should I call?" I replied like a schoolgirl. I passed him my number and his grin made me weak in the knees. I thanked my lucky stars that I was still sitting in my car.

"Well, I'm headed to a Halloween party tonight, but I'll return later if you want to talk then. Call me whenever you get a chance, I'll be ready," he said. "I'm Paxton by the way. It was a pleasure to meet you. I certainly hope that this won't be the last time."

"It won't," I said as I giggled.

We said our goodbyes and he jogged off lightly towards his car. I didn't even notice what type of car it was because I was so busy looking at him. He was FINE!

That's pretty much all that I remember. I am a sucker for a good-looking man. It had been several months since I had even entertained the notion of a man's company. I was immersed in trying to get my life back on track from all of the layers of lies that I had fallen victim to in the past. I was unsure of how to react to the attention of a man that I had not requested. However, I'll admit, I was curious.

By the time I got home and got Talia settled in, the phone rang. It was Paxton.

"Hold on just one second for me, OK?"

"Sure, no problem."

I placed the phone down and began to give myself a pep talk. In that moment, I promised myself that I would not allow myself to be vulnerable. I would not allow myself to be hurt by anyone. I wasn't ready for any more lies and I vowed to myself that I would not put myself in a position to get hurt. I didn't have the strength to go through anything like that again. No more lies.

Paxton and I talked for hours. It seemed like I had the ability to become instant BFF's with people. I had always been a transparent person, sometimes to a fault. That night, we talked about everything — the past, the present, and the future. I made it completely clear that the only thing that I was looking for in him was developing a friendship. He agreed to my terms and we made plans to meet up and hang out.

Our friendship grew as the days passed. We hung out as often as our schedules would allow. I was very serious about my job and achieving new levels of success. My ambition took precedence over everything, except of course Talia because I realized now more than ever that she was my responsibility. There hadn't been much contact between Peter and I, and I had no expectations for his role in our lives.

One afternoon as I was sitting at work, Ms. Waters walked into my office.

"Have you got a minute?"

"Sure, what's up?"

"Well, I've watched you work and I have to say, I knew that you would do an amazing job in this role. It suits you well. I want to offer you a promotion if you would be willing to work with me on acquiring a new property to manage. So, what do you say?"

"YES," I exclaimed. I didn't even know what the new position entailed. I just knew that if it meant making another move upwards, I was ready for it.

"This role will also be an increase in pay, but your hours will remain the same. Additionally, there are some things that can be done from home as well."

I could tell that she was just as excited as I was. I couldn't believe that my life was expanding in ways that I hadn't imagined.

A week after learning of my promotion and new salary, I began searching for an apartment. It was time to create a home of our own. Being a professional in the real estate industry made it so much easier because I had access to all of the best listings. I found a perfect little two bedroom, two and a half bath that was super modern and furnished with new appliances. It was perfect for us. A day later, I scheduled an appointment for a viewing and placed my deposit on the spot. Talia and I were officially starting a life of our own. I did it for us and not one of the men from my past had helped me. Together, we were preparing to write a new chapter.

7: THE BEST THING YOU NEVER HAD

"If they treat you ordinary, don't believe them."

One thing that I learned over the years is that we must be watchful when life is going well. It is in the midst of our most prosperous moments that we forget the tormenting pain of past hurts that became a part of the journey. When we allow ourselves to get comfortable with the patterns that once revealed our inner most desires we become vulnerable beyond repair. I wasn't sure what the road ahead would bring, but I felt a sense of comfort that I had not allowed myself to feel. It was scary but I was willing to enjoy the ride.

LIE #7: FRIENDS WITH BENEFITS CAN BE A BEAUTIFUL THING

On the weekends, Paxton would sit on the stairs that led to my apartment and wait for me. He would wait, sometimes nine or ten hours just to connect with me. I would go to the club with my friends and at two o'clock in the morning, he would always show up with a bottle of wine or some flowers. He never came empty handed. We became genuine friends.

His bald head appeared to be freshly shaven every time that I saw him. He was very fit, with great arms and legs. He also had really nice hands that I grew to fantasize about. The color of his nails was naturally more pink than most men. His nail beds were clean and he kept them well-manicured. He just looked strong, but also beautiful, a combination that I had not yet encountered. When I would see him, my eyes would lock on his arms, not to mention his well-shaped ass. That boy was fine.

Even with his delectable body, it was his charismatic mannerisms that drew me in further. He was the perfect fusion of cocky and confident. He had a way with words that gave him power over people. I would watch him maneuver in stores, and as we would encounter people when we were out.

The more time that I spent with Paxton, the more I discovered how attractive he was. We began to hang out, making runs to the store, the movies, shopping, and sometimes even the club. We had so much fun together!

He even nicknamed me "Rocky," and I thought it was kind of cute.

The more fun that we had, the more I realized just how enticing he was to look at. His personality could draw you in just the same. Women found themselves fanning in his presence; there was just something about him. I could no longer deny my physical attraction towards him. Unless you could control yourself, he would seduce you before you knew it. He was the perfect gentleman. One night after sitting on my steps and talking, we made an agreement that if he was not seeing anyone and I was not seeing anyone, we would have sex with each other.

I soon found out that Paxton had the ability to screw your brains out. Lord! I can still remember the first time that I saw his penis. It curved to the right a little and it was big as hell. I wanted to be close to him and I longed for the feelings that I felt when he held me in the comfort of his arms. His presence always felt like good company.

Paxton continued to visit me as the weeks passed and he always came bearing gifts. One day, there was a knock at my door and as I opened it, he stood there holding a pink bag that revealed six washcloths, six hand towels, and six bath towels. I remember looking at him and wondering why he felt the need to give me towels. Before I could say a word, he whispered in my ear, "I noticed that you needed some new ones". He would leave me boxes of meat on my back step when I wasn't home. Whether it was a pound of ground round or a pound of bacon, he always gave me something that I could use. One Mother's day, he brought me a robe and house shoes and massaged my entire body until I couldn't take anymore. He was consistent and I respected that.

After our nights of passionate sex, Paxton would leave notes lying around my apartment that I would discover the next morning and sometimes days later. He had such a way with words, even in his writing. He was very intelligent and could articulate well. Many nights, we would lay in bed and talk about everything and nothing. Whether discussing politics, sports, or work, he always found some common ground in the discussion. Paxton had so many good qualities that he was almost too good to be true.

Despite all of this, there was always something about him that was off, although I couldn't put my finger on it. Even with all that he had in his favor, I never pursued a relationship with him. I could've given a laundry list as to why I did not want more than just a friendship with benefits with Paxton, but the most compelling was the promise that I had made to myself about being vulnerable and not allowing myself to be hurt. I meant it with everything inside of me that I would not allow myself to fall for anyone the way that I had in the past. I could not stomach that type of pain from the possibilities of deceit again. If I were completely honest, I secretly still wanted to be with Ryan deep down in my heart.

I knew that Paxton was not with me every day or every night for that matter. There were huge blocks of his time that were unaccounted for. I didn't ask. I'm not sure that I wanted to know. I was smart enough to realize that if I saw all of those amazing qualities in him, there had to be others who enjoyed his company the same way that I did. One night in particular, we decided to go out to a club to dance and just hang out. As we walked in, we approached the bar. I never really drank, but I did smoke cigarettes. Lord knows I wanted to stop because I could never seem to shake that image of Barb, my old supervisor, and the effects that cigarettes had on her appearance, but they were my outlet.

As we sat and jammed to the music, Paxton jumped up in a way that I had never seen him jump before. He looked as if he had seen a ghost.

"I'll be right back, you stay here OK?"

"Sure, no problem," I replied. I couldn't have imagined what was wrong. In all the time that we had spent together, I hadn't taken the time to learn too much about his family, or his friends for that matter. I was clueless outside of the bond that he and I shared.

After about twenty minutes of sitting unaccompanied, I decided to walk around the club to see if I could find him. The music was so loud; I could barely hear my thoughts. This nightclub was crowded. Maybe because the weather was so nice, everyone wanted to get out and just live like us. The DJ slowed the tempo a bit by playing a slow song and I could see from my view on the top floor that the dynamics on the dance floor below had changed. People were coming closer together and men and women were holding hands. It was amazing how one song could change the mood for so many people simultaneously. One couple stood out from the rest because they appeared to be exchanging words. The lady looked upset and the gentleman was profusely trying to explain himself. As I got closer to the railing, it became apparent to me that the gentleman was Paxton. I stood there leaning over the railing to observe more. He was entangled in a heated argument with a woman that looked familiar. It was Ms. Waters. How in the hell did Paxton know Ms. Waters and why would they be arguing? Hell, why had he left me at the bar? Was she the reason that he jumped up so abruptly? This was too damn much.

I proceeded towards the steps in a rage. How dare he disrespect me this way. I couldn't believe my eyes. When I got to the dance floor, they were still there, but it seemed as though their argument had subsided. I walked right up to him and tapped him on the shoulder. In that moment, I forgot that Ms. Waters was even my boss.

"Excuse me!" I said in an aggravated tone.

"Here she is. This is who I was telling you about, Babe".

"Babe?" I said. "She's your Babe?"

"Rachel. Girl, it's good to see you. I had no idea that you knew Paxton. The world is so very small," Ms. Waters said.

"Rachel, I see that the two of you know each other already. Melissa is my girlfriend. We've been living together for about eight months now. I told her what an amazing friend you've been to me."

"He spoke of his friend Rocky all the time but I had no clue that it was you. I'm glad to know that he was in good company," she said.

"Rocky, I'm going to make sure that Melissa gets home safely. Would you mind catching a cab back to your apartment?" I will call to check on you tomorrow. You're the best."

Instead of slapping him and throwing my cup of sprite at his face, I smiled and walked away quietly. I no longer had a desire to be there in that moment. I walked immediately to the door and down the street to hail a cab. On the ride home, the silence in the cab was deafening. I couldn't help but think about how amazing I thought Ms. Waters was, or should I say Melissa. I guess he saw the same in her. There was a strange feeling that came over me. How mad could I actually be? Whether I was willing to admit it or not, things had turned out as I predicted and I had not allowed myself to become attached or to fall in love like I had in the past. Hell, I won! If I decided to no longer deal with Paxton, I would not be losing anything. Sure, I would miss our friendship, but I was not reliant on him to be the keeper of my heart. I leaned back in the backseat of the cab and began laughing hysterically. The cab driver seemed startled because the laughter seemed to have come from nowhere. If only he knew that I found victory for the first time in my search for love. Some may not have considered it that way, but I did. I saw the time that I had spent with Paxton for what it was worth and by the time the cab stopped in front of my apartment, my desire to spend any further time with him did as well. I also knew that there was no way that I could maintain anything further with him and still remain in good standing at my job with Ms. Waters. I didn't want to bring harm to my professional growth in any way. I paid my fare, got out, and slammed the door to the cab and my relationship with Paxton.

That night when I went to bed, I slept like a baby. The morning after, I awoke to several messages from Paxton, none of which I cared to return. I did get a small sense of satisfactions knowing that he felt guilty. He admitted it. I mean, we had been such good friends that even he knew he could have disclosed his relationship to me. I don't even believe that it would have really changed much. The deceit that I experienced was in how he handled the night before at the club. It wasn't worth my time to continue thinking about it and I didn't. I got up, went into Talia's room and saw that she was still asleep. That face was my why, and she was all that mattered.

Months passed by and I ceased all communication with Paxton. He left messages here and there, but I never returned his calls. I continued to focus on making a life for Talia and myself. I was making tremendous gains in my new position and the company was the better for it. Things were noticeably different between Ms. Waters and me, but we both recognized the benefit in our working relationship. It was as if she knew more and I knew more, but we had both been deceived and we recognized it. I never referred to her as Melissa because it was important for me to maintain a certain level of professionalism.

About two months after the incident in the club, she called me into her office to tell me that I had reached a new goal and was in consideration for another promotion. I would now be responsible for training other employees in some of the same sales tactics that I had become notorious for. Not only would this be an increase in pay, but also more flexibility with my schedule. My goal would be to work to become tenured with this company, as I had done with the state. It was just the boost that I needed and I was insistent on not being distracted by anyone or anything.

About a week after my new promotion, I received a phone call from my cousin Tracy in Sacramento. I told her of my promotion and she was insistent that we celebrate. She informed me that she and my cousin Macy were coming down to Oakland the following weekend. A week later, I found myself getting dressed up for an evening of fun. We decided to take a leisurely drive around Lake Merritt. It was a very popular hangout in the middle of the city. In the evenings, the cars would be out and so were the men. A girl couldn't help but notice.

Nice cars always equal men. It seemed that everyone was in a flirtatious mood. We joked the entire evening as we people watched, and found a source of laughter in comparing the different men who accompanied the cars that they had invested so much time and money in fixing up. Quality time with them was just what I needed to unwind. I guess I had been somewhat uptight since the incident and as much as I didn't want to admit that it bothered me, I did feel like I hadn't been picked. What the hell?

I wasn't about to let thoughts of Paxton, or anyone else, ruin my evening with the girls for a single minute. Today was about us and celebrating my new promotion. After leaving the park, we stopped to get gas before heading out for our next adventure. As Tracy pulled around to the pump closest to the front door of the store, I saw a familiar face.

"It can't be," I said in a startled voice.

Tracy got out to pump the gas and I heard her shriek, "What are you doing here?"

I dropped my head in dismay. It was Ryan. I could recognize his massive physique anywhere. I couldn't believe my eyes.

"I guess I should ask you the same thing, Tracy," he said jokingly. As he walked over to the car, he appeared to be looking for me. "Is she in there?" he asked.

"She sure is," Tracy said as she burst into laughter.

"Oh my God girl, what are you going to say?" asked Macy.

"Girl, I don't know. Damn!"

"What are you doing here? Get out and give me a hug girl," he said. "You are looking good.

"Thanks Ryan. You look nice too." Before I knew it, I blurted out "You should come over and see my place."

"I'd love to!" he said with an evil grin.

I gave him my address and well, I'm not sure if I thought that he would come, but the damage was potentially done now. We said our goodbyes and Ryan gestured with his lips that he would see me later.

"Girl, you are in trouble tonight," said Macy.

The entire car burst into laughter. I wasn't sure if Macy would be right, but we enjoyed the rest of our evening by going to a Mexican restaurant that I had always wanted to try. It was ironic that we chose that place, especially considering that Ryan was half Mexican and it had been such a point of contention.

After the girls dropped me off, they decided to go out to hang some more. Talia was with my aunt so I had the house to myself. Sure enough, a little less than an hour after being home, Ryan called. We picked up right where we left off. He made love to me like he truly loved me. My love for him never left and all of the feelings that I had tried to put aside were resurrected. We held each other for a few hours and then he hit the road to go back to Sacramento. I remember standing at the front door hoping that I could leave the night right where it was and not expect something more to develop. I took a shower and thought to myself that nothing was promised to me.

About an hour later, I received an unexpected call from a number that I didn't recognize. I thought that maybe it was Tracy and Macy letting me know about their escapades in Oakland.

"Hello?" I said.

"Rachel, it's me. It has been way too long. You can't still be mad at me. I miss you. I just bought a new car and I am dying for you to see it. I'm on my way over," he said.

It was Paxton. How in the hell did I go from spending countless nights alone, to having the company of two men in the same night? Where and when does this ever happen?

When Paxton pulled up, I opened the door and he was standing in front of the car looking like a damn snack. He was so freakin gorgeous. His smile seemed to light up the night. His new car was a white Diamante. It had four doors and a beautiful peanut butter interior. It suited him perfectly. Just like old times, we stood there talking for hours. Neither of us spoke of what happened that night with Ms. Waters. I guess it was water under the bridge. She was still my boss so I was reluctant to say much.

We began laughing as we had always done about and in the midst of doing so, he pulled me close to him and I could feel his nature rising.

"You know I never meant to hurt you, right?"

I was torn.

"Why don't you let me come inside?"

I wanted him as much as he wanted me in that moment. The same night that I had just rekindled my love with Ryan, Paxton came in for a nightcap and one thing led to another and we hooked up. I can't lie and say that I wasn't satisfied. We had wild, crazy, sex. There was no one there to hear me scream or to interrupt the sound of the headboard against the wall. He knew how to hold me. He knew how to arouse me in ways that I never knew were possible. I didn't regret it. After the night ended, I arose to the morning sun and the same series of handwritten notes that I had come to enjoy so much. He had slipped out while I was asleep and that was fine with me.

After my weekend rendezvous with Ryan and Paxton on the same night, you would think that one, or both of them, would magically reappeared to profess their love and sweep me off my feet with a romantic proposal that every girl dreams of, or at least the prospect of a committed relationship. Quite the contrary.

The real truth is that a month passed by and I didn't heard from either of them. Trust me when I say that I wasn't crushed. I remained focused on chasing my dreams of success. Talia and I were thriving, no thanks to either of them. This was my life and I was living it to the fullest. Around the same time, I was coming close to reaching the one year anniversary of working with Ms. Waters and all I could see was success in my future.

The company had been planning their massive annual outing where new employees were recognized and employees who had been with the company rewarded for various milestones. I was feeling a little more tired, but of course it was because I was pushing myself to the max. I wanted the Employee of the Year Award; it had my name written all over it. Ms. Waters requested that our team wear white to the event. I searched through my closet for a white dress that I had purchased when I first got the job, but never had a reason to wear. It was fitted and I had the perfect pair of heels with a pop of color to wear with it. It was tucked away so far that I barely noticed it behind an old white blouse that I never wore. I pulled it out and admired it on the hanger. After trying to zip it up, I noticed that it was a little more snug then when I had first purchased it. I hadn't remembered gaining any extra weight, but it was a year ago. I tried to keep that kind of thing under control. I attended exercise classes regularly, but I had missed a few because I had opted to come home and take a nap before picking up Talia from her babysitter.

Another week had passed and I was now desperate to find something to wear to the company event. One day, I went out shopping and because I was petite, I never had a problem finding things that fit. They weren't always the selections that I wanted, but there was always something that fit. Today, that was not the case. Nothing in my size fit. I stood in the dressing room feeling concerned. How could I explain the unexpected weight gain? I sat on the small bench facing the mirror in the dressing room staring at myself. Something was different. The more I looked at my reflection, the more I grew concerned. A sense of familiarity came over me. I had been here before. I pulled out my phone to look at the calendar and realized that not only was I tired more often, gaining weight unexplainably, but also that my period was late. It couldn't be, I thought to myself. Was I pregnant? How was this possible? Well, I mean, I know how it was possible — but pregnant?

At what point can we get expect reprieve from the patterns that shape our behaviors? Could life be a series of self-inflicted pain or just the by-product of a predestined evolution? We must learn to not only accept the unchartered paths that reveal themselves to us, but also embrace them. For what lies ahead is called destiny.

$\mathcal{8}$: NEVER SAY NEVER

"It's not possible to find the right person, if you are unwilling to let go of the wrong one."

It's been said, "Sometimes things fall apart so that they can fall together." What does that even mean? Why do things fall apart in the first place? I wish that someone could help me to predict when the pieces of my life will fall apart so that I can prepare for it. I imagine that this dance that we do is all a part of the very intricate journey along a path that we call life.

LIE #8: IT'S NOT WHAT YOU THINK

I rushed home from the store in frustration after nothing that I tried on seemed to fit. I stopped by a drugstore to pick up a pregnancy test. I was almost sure that something else had to be going on. I guess at the time I was in denial. Twenty minutes later, I was peeing on a stick. Ten minutes later, I was sitting in the bay window of my apartment, perplexed and pregnant. I was in an absolute state of shock. I know you're thinking that I should not have been, but trust me when I say that I was. It was the last thing that I had expected.

I knew that I had to let Ryan know that I was pregnant with his child. I reached for the phone as I sat with my pants unbuttoned. It seems like the moment you find out that you are pregnant, you gain an extra ten pounds on the spot.

"H..hello, Ryan. How's everything going? That's good. I . . . I was just calling to let you know that my period was late this month and . . . I took a pregnancy test and . . . I'm pregnant." There was a long moment of silence on the other end. Hell, I didn't know what else to say myself. "Are you still there?" I asked.

"You know what? The right thing for me to do is to step up to the plate and take care of it. I want you to pack up and move back here to Sacramento."

"Wha . . . What? You want me to move in with you?"

"Yes. I will come down this weekend and help you pack and bring you back here. We will do this together," he said.

When I hung up the phone, I was ecstatic. I had always wanted to be with Ryan. If I had known that all it would have taken was for us to start a family, I would have done so more quickly. For him and the family I had always dreamed of, I was willing to give up all that I had worked for. All that I had ever wanted was to experience love like this. As much as I was ambitious, love overruled it all.

Two days later, I submitted my letter of resignation to Ms. Waters. As I sat in her office, I reflected for a moment about how much I was actually willing to give up. I had increased my salary from $50,000 to $60,000 per year. I had an amazing health benefits plan that was sufficient for Talia and myself, paid vacation time, and a company match investment program. None of these were options that had ever been offered to me working for the state. I informed her of my pregnancy with Ryan. Our conversation upon my exit was much like our conversation upon my entrance during my initial interview with the company. She was sad to see me go and I was a little sad to leave, but we both knew that I was being given the opportunity that every woman dreams of — to be married.

Ryan arrived on Friday and my Aunt Mattie, both my sisters, and Ryan packed the whole house. You would have thought that I was nine months pregnant. They didn't let me lift a finger. That evening, we drove to Sacramento with a trailer on the back of Ryan's truck to begin a new life together.

The following Monday, I reinstated my job with the state. Having started my career at such a young age was a plus as it afforded me opportunities like this to leave and return as I did. My experience was of value. I left all of the fancy clothes that I had bought for the real estate industry in the packing box. It was sad to retire them, but the state uniform, which I was allowed to leave untucked, accommodated my growing baby bump.

Ryan promise that we would get married immediately and we did. I guess you could call it a shotgun wedding at the courthouse, but it meant so much to me that we would welcome our child as a family who was bound by love.

As the days passed, I grew more and more excited. Ryan was so good to me. Our hours were very similar, as we were both working at the department of corrections. This allowed us to drive to and from work together. We bonded like old times and I worked hard to understand what he wanted emotionally and physically in a wife. For the first time in a long time, I felt like somebody wanted to be with me for who I was, and it meant the world to me.

Ryan and I became heavily involved in the apostolic faith, and together we began attending his mother's church again. We were so happy to reunite. She was thrilled at the prospect of having another grandchild, as she had already considered Talia to be her granddaughter. Life was simple and that was good enough for me.

I would've done just about anything to be what Ryan wanted and needed me to be. We grew deeper together in our spiritual walk. We represented the old apostolic church and abided by the rules as such. In the faith, there were many limitation that I was not accustomed to. We couldn't wear short sleeve shirts or have skirt hemlines above the knee. These didn't affect me much since I felt so much larger when carrying the baby. I was happy to cover up. The more difficult rules, which sometimes led me to feel trapped, were that we weren't allowed to watch TV or listen to secular music. However, at the time, this was the life that I had dreamed of with Ryan.

There was still a part of me that needed justification for the motives that governed the ordained rules. I was always curious about everything. Why weren't we able to watch TV? I loved the rap artist Tupac. Why was I forbidden from enjoying his music? You could not convince me that if I listened to Tupac, I was going to hell for it. I just didn't believe that to be true. To me, being Godly was more about how you treated people and the good that you did in the world than abiding by rules that you ultimately couldn't explain. We would meet other couples who were part of the religion and some would go as far as to not buy wedding rings in an attempt to maintain the minimalist lifestyle that the religion called for. I couldn't understand how someone wouldn't invest in wedding rings, but have on a Gucci watch? How was it that TV was forbidden, but many of the couples kept a

small TV in their bedrooms? There were so many incon-
sistencies that made me question the religious practices,
but I loved God and Ryan without question in my heart.
I just didn't understand the man made rules that were a
part of what Ryan and I practiced.

My belly kept growing and so did our walk together
into parenthood. Ryan was an amazing father to Talia.
He stepped right in and never missed a beat. He read to
her and spent time playing games with her. He got all of
the practice that he would ever need before our new baby
was born. In retrospect, I recognize that there was not a
whole lot of time for us. Like most couples, everything
was centered around children and work.

I worked every day until going into labor. My water
broke while out on a lunch break and I called Ryan, who
met me and drove me to the hospital. We were having
a baby. Showtime!

McKenzie Alicia Suarez was born on the eighth day of
July at 7:43 p.m. She weighed six pounds, seven ounces.
That child was born smiling, I swear. She was the hap-
piest baby. I now had two girls to share in the joy of life
with me. My Talia and McKenzie became my heart's
desire. I had no idea that my heart had the capacity to
love so much.

Ryan shared in my sentiment and was determined to
be the best father that he could be. He decided to take
a leave from work to spend time with the girls and so
that McKenzie would not have to go to daycare after I

returned to work. When I say that he was all in, he was all in. He even had a fanny pack with the newborn items on the front to be prepared for whatever she may have needed. It was black leather and he looked like a fool wearing it, but he was my fool and I loved him for it. I had never seen a man be so enthusiastic about nurturing his newborn child. It was a love that I hadn't seen.

Ryan and I were like ships in passing. Sleepless nights, bottles, sexless days, and lethargy were our new normal. I had experienced this somewhat when I had Talia. It was different experiencing it with Ryan. Our routines consisted of work, grocery store, church and more work for me. I could tell by his temperament that Ryan was getting a little tired of remaining at home. He found great joy in working and creating a way of life for his family. Even though he had opted for paternity leave, it wouldn't be long before he would desire to return to work. After three months of nonstop daddy duty, Ryan took a position with the state, working the night shift at a juvenile detention hall.

I wanted to do all that I could to continue to build a family with him and be the wife that I thought he desired. I would take him plates of food to his job, write little notes and leave them placed in his bag, and even try to surprise him on the job with visits from me if I could get the neighbor to keep an eye on the kids for a half an hour or so. Sometimes, when I would go to Ryan's job, I would bring the children with me. Due to the security of the location, you had to be buzzed in, which often made the element of surprise fizzle, but I gave it my best shot.

There was one co-worker in particular who always seemed to be waiting for me when I arrived. She was very kind and always so complimentary of me. Every time she would open the door, she would compliment me. She would say things like, "Oh your hair is cute," or "I love that blouse," or "Your baby is beautiful." I later learned that her name was Tamar. Woman to woman, I appreciated her kind words. After having a baby, there are times when you don't feel as though you look your best, but I desperately wanted to for Ryan.

Although extremely nice, there was something about Tamar that didn't quite sit well with me. I blamed my feelings on low self-esteem and hormones. We all know that having a baby will do that to you. Furthermore, I was still trying to satisfy Ryan with the appropriate clothes to honor our spiritual walk. To be honest, and I truly mean no harm, I felt like we looked like Pilgrims. How the hell was Tamar complimenting me when I was dressed as if I had just stepped off the Mayflower? Truthfully, it didn't matter; I needed to hear it from someone because I wasn't hearing it from Ryan at home.

As the months passed by, Ryan and I began to see some consistency with his schedule. I worked during the day and he worked at night. We would spend extended time with each other on Tuesdays and Thursdays on the drive to his mother's church. That was our time when we caught up on everything. We talked about a great deal of nothing and that was OK with us. It was always very surface and never too deep. Quite frankly, those were the only moments of quality time that we spent together. One Friday, Ryan called me and told me that he would need to work late. I never asked questions. I accepted whatever he said. I trusted him to do what he felt was best for all of us. On this day in particular, I remember rolling my eyes because I had gone out of my way to plan a candlelit dinner for him when he arrived at home. I had even done something different with my hair. I just wanted him to compliment me, to notice me. I decided that since he wouldn't be able to see the surprise that I had at home for him, I would do what I could to surprise him at his job with the special plate of steak, potatoes, and green bean casserole that I had prepared. It was his favorite meal. After arriving, I rang the doorbell and like clockwork, Tamar answered the door. She looked surprised that I was present.

"H . . . h . . . hello, Mrs. Suarez." There was something different about her demeanor, but I couldn't quite put my finger on it, nor did I have time to. Over time, I felt like she paid attention to me in a different way. Here compliments continued, but I couldn't help but notice that the tone had changed. It was almost as if she felt like I was a bother when I came to the job. There was an undertone of sarcasm that accompanied her voice.

It was never enough for me to actually say anything about it because it would have made me appear petty and with two children, a husband, and a job, I had no time to be petty.

After visiting, one evening, I finally found the insight to verbalize what I had been sensing about Tamar. As Ryan walked me to my car, away from the building, I looked at him and said, "That girl that keeps answering the door, she is your type." His response was nothing that startled me in any way.

"I don't know what you are talking about," he said.

I wasn't threatened. I was the wife. My security was in what we were building together. She was just another worker on the shift and although I felt like I needed to keep one eye open for her, I wasn't worried.

The more Ryan worked, the more he desired to work. There was really no us, and the time and distance made me feel alone. I could sense that he was not happy, but who would be while working so many hours? I attributed it to his work ethic that he had come to embody for his family. If he didn't love us, he wouldn't work so hard to support us. He must have been working at least eighty hours a week by now. It took a toll on us. He was never there. Finally, I asked him if he wanted to go to counseling. I figured that we needed more than just the car rides twice a week to keep us going. Maybe a controlled environment would give us a better chance to talk than we had been able to give ourselves. His willingness to go was just another sign of his dedication to the relationship and us. Where I come from, men are not really open to the idea of a counselor and "working through" things. He was. He didn't hesitate when asked.

Sadly, I have to admit that even after months of counseling, nothing changed. We were in a stalemate. Even my visits to his job had become so routine that there was no excitement about going. I wasn't remotely excited to visit him. I loved him with my whole heart, but there was no romance and I'm not sure I can honestly say that we were in love. I didn't miss him when he was away. It seemed to be more work when he was around because everything was contrived and forced. How had we gotten to this place?

It was inevitable that Ryan and I were nearing the end of our marriage. McKenzie was a little over one year old. We amicably separated and I moved out of our home into a condo. We were still going to marriage counseling, trying to figure out if the marriage was salvageable.

Call it paranoia, but in the back of my mind, I couldn't help but wonder if Tamar had anything to do with Ryan's distance from me? Let's not pretend that I hadn't previously experienced the lies men tell. What I will say is that a woman's intuition, when turned on makes her an automatic detective with the ability to solve mysteries that seemed to be cold. It was now my belief that I had one to crack right under my nose. Even though we were not technically together, Ryan was still my husband and we were still trying to work it out, but I was curious.

I had managed to crack the code to his voicemail and access his calling list. As I lay in my bed at the condo, I checked his voicemail. I heard a voice say, "I'm on my way. I will be there soon." It was Tamar, and to make matters worse, it was late as hell at night. I could recognize her voice anywhere. She had spoken to me too many times. Why would she be going over to his house at this hour?

I had to see with my own eyes. The voicemail alone was not enough. I jumped up and threw some pajamas on the girls. Damn right, they were coming with me. I pulled through the McDonald's drive through and bought them each a happy meal and then parked my car right in front of Ryan's house. I didn't see anything suspicious. I'm sure you're thinking that most would have just done a drive by. Not me. If I had gone through the trouble to get my babies up and in the backseat, I was going to find out all that I could. I had to know. It was killing me.

Do you know what it's like to think that you are crazy? Have you ever been made to feel that it's just you who is not right in the relationship? That was what I was feeling and continually, I blamed myself for the unraveling of us. If that was not the case and he had been cheating, I needed to know. I deserved to know. With my kids in tow, I was in a full fledge stake out.

Talia asked, "Mommy, why are we here now?"

"I think Mr. Ryan is doing something bad and I am going to find out," I replied.

Before I could turn around to look back towards the house, Talia exclaimed, "Mommy, I think I see somebody up there."

Low and behold, Ryan was coming down the stairs and towards the front door. I knew the house and his movements in it very well. It was my damn house! Before I knew it, I hopped out of the car and after getting just to the middle of the street, instructed the girls to stay put. When he opened the door, I pushed past him like I was the FBI. I ran up the stairs like a mad woman. I was slamming doors, opening closets, scaling the hallways, peeking in the bathrooms; I wanted to find that bitch.

"What's wrong with you?" Ryan said.

We met in the upstairs hallway that led towards the bathroom. I ran past him, back down the stairs toward the kitchen sink. It was the only place I hadn't yet looked. Now would a grown ass women really be under the kitchen sink? In the moment, I thought anything was possible. I stopped dead in my tracks and picked up a vase filled with an old flower bouquet and I screeched at him, "I will kill you before I let you cheat on me Ryan."

"Rachel, if you don't stop it right now, I promise, that I will call the police. I swear. I will do it now." The thunder in his voice snapped me back to reality. Again, I was forced to believe that I was losing my mind. I bowed my head in shame and began to walk out in a different manner. I was defeated.

As I walked down the stairs, I could see my shadow on the ground in the night's reflection. I heard a motor running. I lifted my head and from the darkness of the night, emerged Tamar. She and her friend had pulled up in a white car. I looked to see if my girls were still safe and secure in the car and they were. I looked over at Tamar to ensure that she saw me and then I proceeded to get in the car and start the ignition. With tears streaming down my face, I backed up the car so that I was directly in front of Ryan's house. I needed to look Tamar square in the eyes.

"I'll be goddamned, Tamar. You are asking for me to beat your ass, Bitch."

For some reason, all I could see were her titties. She had these big perky titties that pissed me off even more. Here I was, sitting with boobs bearing war wounds from two kids, dressed in jammies, in a car that smelled like goddamn happy meals, lonely, confused, and abandoned, and this bitch was sneaking to my husband's house with perky titties? What kind of karma was this?

"You are my husband's subordinate and you're out here at my husband's house at this hour? I knew all along that you wanted him. That's it Bitch. It's me and you."

"I will call the police," I heard a voice yell from inside the house. It was Ryan. How could a husband be willing to call the police on his wife for confronting his mistress? It was all fucked up. I no longer wanted my daughters to bear witness to me being demeaned. I would never want them to find themselves in the predicament that I found myself in. I secured my babies and drove home.

When I arrived back at the condo, I unloaded the girls and tucked them safely in their beds. If I had been a drinker, I would have grabbed a glass of wine. Instead, I smoked a cigarette to calm me down. I was full of rage that had no escape. My heart was heavy, my mind was racing, and my soul was shattered. A few minutes later, there was a knock at the door. It was a female police officer.

"Ma'am, I received a call about a disturbance at a residence not far from here. Is everything OK?"

With tears in my eyes, I looked her square in the eyes and said, "Everything is not OK. I just found out that my husband has been cheating on me and I'm mad as hell." My voice was trembling.

"I'm sorry to hear that ma'am. I truly am, but we need for you to remain peaceful and not cause any danger to yourself or anyone else. Is that understood?"

I nodded my head in defeat.

"I would just advise that you do not go back there, Ma'am."

"Don't worry, I won't." Although the officer had no certainty of this, I had no plans of ever returning to that house or to Ryan.

This was the ultimate crash and burn saga for me. All I had ever done was try to love Ryan. All I had ever done was try to love Paxton. All I had ever done was try to love Desmond. All I had ever done was try to love Peter. What I had gotten in exchange for love was a series of breaks, fractures, and tears to my heart. I was beyond the point of being mended. I was bound, broke, and wrapped in chains.

9: WOMAN, THOU ART LOOSED

"What would happen if everyone simply told the truth?"

There is so much that is revealed in truth, but we often choose to live amidst the lies. There are times when the comfort of a lie feels better than the power of truth. I lived engulfed in the comfort of lies. Lies that I told myself and lies that I allowed myself to believe. The blanket of lies suffocated me to the point that I believed it normal. In the end, we must decide between the breath of life or the lies of death and self-destruction.

LIE #9: IF YOU LOVE SOMETHING, YOU SHOULD SET IT FREE.

After discovering that Ryan had been cheating on me all along with Tamar, and that he chose to protect what he had with her over our family, I was broken in places that

I never even knew existed. I lost my sense of purpose. I forgot who I was and what I wanted to see manifest in my life. My ambition was compromised and there was a dull pain in the depths of my soul that I couldn't seem to remedy. I was strong enough to know that my life was worth living, but I couldn't dig deep enough to find my why. In those moments of desperation that evolved into years of pain, I honestly thought that God had forgotten about me. The religion I worked so hard to practice, that we had built a life around, was nowhere to be found. I lost so much respect for him as he had been the spiritual leader of our household and when the light shined in the darkness, it revealed that he was the one who couldn't be trusted. I was left with no other choice than to file for divorce.

Throughout the process of severing our ties, I was forced to step outside of my body to find purpose. I discovered that if for no other reason, I woke up each day to ensure that Talia and Mackenzie had the very best that I could give them. I owed them my best because they had not asked to come into the world. I found great pride in ensuring that their lives didn't skip a beat. Although I was hurting tremendously on the inside, they brought great joy, and in their smiles I discovered strength that I didn't know I possessed.

Over time, Tamar became more visible. As if the picture could have been painted any clearer, Ryan eventually showed her off as his girlfriend, without apology. Not long after their relationship was public, that bitch became his fiancé. And while I'm all for women's empowerment, I feel well within my rights to refer to her as a bitch because that is exactly how she acted. She plotted and strategized the best way to get my husband. Although I don't shy away from any of my part in why our relationship did not work, I held her responsible for tearing my family apart. I'm sure if she were asked, she would never admit it, but I know the truth, we all do. As long as I have breath in my body, I will speak on the insurmountable pain that was caused. I would never wish such torment upon another woman. Tamar went after my husband and she took him. These are the facts. Today, I wish her the best, she can most definitely have his ass, but I can't pretend that it didn't hurt like hell. If I were allowed a truth moment, I'd tell you that in my heart I hated her. I know that it is a strong word, but it was my truth. Because of what I had experienced with Ryan and Tamar, I walked the tightrope of temporary insanity. The loss of my marriage impacted my self-esteem, actions, and perception of life in general. Ryan and I were not casually dating; we were married with children. Even though we had experienced our fair share of ups and downs, I could not for the life of me understand why Ryan would compromise our family.

In order for you to understand what I went through, you have to go down in the valley with me. I was tormented by feelings of inadequacy. When I was with Ryan,

I blamed myself for being suspicious. I blamed myself for what was not going well in our marriage and I even blamed myself for its demise. I carried the weight, the burden of someone else's decision to cheat. I owned it. Maybe, if I had prayed harder, fought harder, loved harder, our relationship could have withstood the test of time. At times, the valley's got to be too much. Eventually, I entered into a never-ending phase of attempting to change or fix everything about myself. I cut all of my hair off, not quite Britney Spears, but damn near close. I went and got braces, and I started losing weight. I figured that if I looked my best, the pain would go away. I was trying to heal myself from the outside in. No one ever spoke of this pain to me. No one ever told me that I needed to heal from the inside out. To make matters worse, I had to interact with Ryan and Tamar and watch them build a life together. Ryan was very much a father to McKenzie. I hated him so much that I wanted to pack up both of my babies and drive away into the sunset, never to return again, but I never could have done that to a father who wanted to be involved in his child's life. I gave it the good old college try to be amicable with them, but they consumed me. I was on an emotional roller coaster and it didn't seem that I would be exiting any time soon. On a good day, I wanted to be cool with them in hopes that I was mature enough to move past the hurt, sit on a beach amidst a blended family, and sing kumbaya. On other days, I literally wanted to set their house on fire.

After all, it was my old house and my old life that she was living. They didn't even have the decency to move out of our old home. It was as if what Ryan and I had was a pencil drawing and I was just erased out. To add insult to injury, when McKenzie would go over to visit, it was as if they had the perfect little family. I was now the single mom outsider, struggling to make ends meet and they were playing house with two solid incomes with my kid to boot. It absolutely crushed my spirits. I kept trying to tell myself that I would be OK. That was the biggest lie ever. I walked through life amidst depression for the next seven years.

I was unstable, not to the point of not caring adequately for my girls, but to the point of not caring adequately for myself. The sad part is, I'm not alone. There are so many women like me who can't seem to pick up the pieces to empower themselves, but never miss a beat to give their children the world. The world is filled with so much unnecessary pain and I carried more than my fair share. My outlook was so poor that, I even considered taking my life. Seeing them together made me sick to my stomach. My days and nights were consumed with what they were doing, what changes they were making to my house, and how they were loving. I couldn't help but wonder what she had that I didn't. And even after all that Ryan had put me through, I still felt a sense of competition with Tamar. The world tells us that the mistress never wins. That was another lie. That bitch stole my life and was living it to the fullest, or at least that's what it looked like. I had to know why Ryan had chosen her over me.

While in the valley, there were also moments of desperation. I had convinced myself that forgiveness from Ryan would make me happy. I was seeking forgiveness for any pain that I had caused him through the years. I also wanted forgiveness for not fighting harder for us. I know it sounds crazy, but when you are insane, nothing quite seems to make sense. One day, as I was sitting in my condo peering out of my bay window, I picked up the phone and dialed Ryan's number.

"Hello," he said in a startled manner. I never called him, unless there was a significant emergency about McKenzie, but on this day, that wasn't the case.

"Ryan, I just wanted to tell you that I am sorry for any part that I played in our love not lasting. It truly broke my heart". Here I was professing my love to him again. In that moment, I realized how deeply I felt for him.

"Come over. Just come over, I need to see you," he said.

I could tell that in that moment, we connected as we had when we were just dating. I could hear in his voice that he had forgotten who Tamar was, even if it was temporary. I got in my car and drove to my former home. I had to see if he had ever loved me. I needed to feel his touch. I needed to be caressed by his hands. I longed to wrap my arms around his wide back. Before I could open my car door, he was standing at the front door of the house. We made love in our bed that he and Tamar now shared. In the heat of the passion, neither one of us thought about Tamar or anyone else for that matter. He made love to me like he used to. He gazed into my eyes like I had always dreamed of. I hadn't known this Ryan. He had never quite let me in. This was the Ryan that I had hoped for my entire life. We laid in bed for a short period of time and just talked. He eventually told me that he understood why I was angry. Although it wasn't quite an apology, I left my former home feeling like I had a small victory. To this day, I have no idea where Tamar was and frankly, my dear, I don't give a damn.

Ryan and I never spoke of that day, but for me it represented the closure of yet another chapter.

The day after Ryan and I made love, I had no remorse. I didn't see it as sleeping with her fiance because he was technically still my husband. I can't even say that at that point I thought that it would rekindle anything between us. I just benefitted from the satisfaction of knowing that he was aware that he had hurt me, and that he was in some manner apologetic. I felt nothing towards her because she had exercised no regard towards me.

One day, after dropping McKenzie off to Ryan and Tamar, I sat in my car and cried. I couldn't believe that they got to have the family that I had worked to create. As I sat in the car, I began to journal my thoughts. I felt as though the paper was the only thing that would listen to me. Over the years, I had talked to family and friends, but nothing seemed to help and after so many years of agonizing, people really believe that you should get over it and move on. The days turned into months and the months turned into years. I didn't officially file for divorce until seven years after I drove away from my house, with the horror of knowing that another woman would be taking up residence there with my husband. For seven years, I pretended to be OK on the outside, but I agonized in my private moments. He never filed because he had no need to. Tamar was playing house with him just fine.

When the divorce proceedings were in full force, it resurrected a great deal of pain that I had believed I had worked through. We were now all amicable, but I was numb to both of them. My only concern was that my daughter be treated fairly when in their care.

I found out during that time, that the night when I caught Tamar at the house, Ryan had actually attempted to press charges on me. That made me angry, but it was also a moment of acceptance that he simply chose her over me. That might have been the hardest pill to swallow and even though they had been parading it around in my face for all of those years, I decided to accept it. It seemed as though the walls were closing in and for me there would be no reprieve. I can admit over the seven years that Ryan and I had not filed, I hated Tamar. I never once believed that she was more at fault than he was; I just knew that she plotted to destroy my family.

That offense was unforgivable. Life and the way that it unravels is peculiar in many ways. I needed those years to gain enough strength to face them as a team in court. So much had happened and I would have never imagined that I would need to prepare for what would unfold.

To relinquish the hurt, and to make myself stronger by making peace with the pain, I wrote a letter directly to Tamar. I never planned to share it with anyone, but it was very meaningful to me.

Dear Tamar,

Allow me to start by saying that this is between you and me. It is my belief that when a woman has a concern with another, the discussion must be woman to woman. So, woman to woman, I must admit that my heart is disappointed in you. My soul aches due to the pain that you caused me. I know without question that you could have taken the time and exerted a little more energy into discovering a love of your own. It saddens me that you felt it necessary to duplicate the blueprint that was already being constructed for my life. Woman to woman, I believe you to be weak for that decision. What I will say is that it was your choice. Every day, we suit up and go out into the world preparing for battle. We are all required to face something. Never in a million years did I think that my war would be with you. I also realize that you came to war, prepared for for it. I came to the battled armed with only love. Today, I realize that we are two different women and our wars are two different wars. Instead of fighting you, I stand in the midst of the battlefield fighting for myself. I own this mission and want nothing more than to simply be happy. I recognize now more than ever that if a man was truly who he revealed himself to be and worthy of my love, I would need no ammunition, as there would be no war to fight.

I realize today that I could have never been what Ryan truly wanted, and I can honestly say that I don't want to be. It no longer hurts me to say that I believe that you deserve each other. I just know that I deserve better and my daughters deserve better. The clearest of indications of this is in the fact that even today, you would rather let me believe that I was wrong about your affair during our marriage. Woman to woman, that is so uncouth.

All I ever wanted was an apology. That was then. This is now, and one is not required.

Today, I am healed. I have grown tremendously and I have the pain to thank. I've learned to seize the opportunities that life presented me, to focus on the betterment of me. And as much as this may seem strange, I sincerely wish you both a blessed life together. Woman to woman, I give you miracles and blessings.

You see, in the midst of the pain, I've forgotten about you because I was introduced to myself. Today, I am beyond happy because I released myself from all of the hurt, and all of the pain, and all of the guilt. Most importantly, I am happy with the woman that I see in the mirror. I didn't know my own strength, but because of this, because of you, I learned how much I could endure. I will forever be grateful for the many lessons that life has taught me and I will maintain a special place in my heart for the pain that taught me that the greatest battle is fought and won within. Woman to woman, I wish you well and I do pray that someday, if not today, you too will look in the mirror and love the reflection that you see.

With Sincerity,
RL

Writing that letter set me free. Prior to that time, I hadn't even been able to identify the bondage that hindered me for so many years. Even my daughters recognized a change in my perspective.

One day after picking up McKenzie, Talia started a conversation, "Mom, I think Tamar is wondering why you don't care about what they are doing anymore."

I couldn't believe the words that this smart, intuitive, young soul had produced. "What do you mean?" I questioned

"Well, it just seems that you are not concerned about them like you used to be and it seems like it bothers her. When I go over or run in to pick up McKenzie, she asks questions like, 'Did your mom say anything?' or 'Did your mom wear pajamas again to pick you guys up?' I can tell that it concerns her because it seems like you are doing better."

In that moment, I cried tears of release. Both of my girls recognized that I had spent so much of my time worrying about Ryan and Tamar that I never stopped to think that just maybe they enjoyed the attention that I had given to them. In retrospect, I recognize that people can look at your mannerisms and know that you care. If Talia hadn't said that, I would have never thought from that perspective.

From that day forward, a new movement was initiated. It was a reflection of how much I had given. I was like, "Wow, I've been singing and dancing for them for seven years." I also began to recognize some familiar patterns of my past. I had been told by two different men who cheated on me that they would call the police on me for being irrational. What the hell was that about? I now recognized that when love has left the building, we must also learn to walk away.

I was now well enough to call my feelings by name. In the midst of the pain, I had low self-esteem, I felt lost, I felt cheated, I felt abandoned, I felt lied to, and I felt afraid. In retrospect, I should have taken that energy that I put towards loving men who didn't love me back, and put it towards healing myself. I hadn't known any better. That was no longer the case.

I rekindled my romance with ambition and started becoming very goal oriented. It occurred to me that from the time that I had enrolled in college — just before Peter and I separated, to now — that I had taken classes for twelve years with no completion. It would stop and start based on whatever was happening with the men in my life. My worst interruptions involved Ryan. If I saw him, I would drop all of my classes and I wasted so much of my time and money. No longer. I realized that the goals that I set for myself were for me and no one else. It was time for a new chapter and I was going to write this one my way and on my terms.

And when it all comes crashing down — stand. Never allow what you are going through to determine your final destination. Test your strength, push your boundaries, remain vigilant under pressure; after all, it is what reveals the diamond in the ruff. I no longer believe that if you love something, you should set it free. If it was ever yours, it would never desire to be anywhere except captivated by your love. If it ever desires to be free, it was not yours to love. And that's the damn truth.

10: EXPECT THE UNEXPECTED

*"It is indeed the unexpected that shifts the atmosphere
and changes our lives."*

The ups and downs and the highs and lows of life create
those butterflies that we often feel in our stomachs because
we are indeed riding a never-ending roller coaster. That
means moments of thrill and excitement, and moments
of terror for what will be. Either way, it will always be
in our best interest to enjoy the ride.

LIE #10: PEOPLE CHANGE

After a seven-year hiatus from loving myself, I had some
serious work to do. The proceedings of the divorce no
longer fazed me. There was so much back and forth and
it seemed like it was taking forever. I just wanted it to
be over. It was confusing to me as to why the divorce

settlement took so long. Ryan did not have anything for me to fight about, he wasn't rich, nor was I. We were two people trying to create a life and a family. The most tumultuous part of the process was making decisions regarding McKenzie. She was now eight years old. Our arrangement at the time was that they had weekend visitation and every other holiday. I started to believe that they wanted much more. They began to tear apart my character and threw accusations as if I was an unfit mother. They were after full custody. I knew that I had been fighting to keep my head above water emotionally, but at no point in time was I an unfit mother. My girls never went without their needs being met. I had managed to build a wall of resistance against anything that they attempted to do to hurt me and I was most certainly not going to let their daggers strike my daughters.

Even though court was now a constant fight, I was still determined to get back to me. Love was the absolute last thing that I was in search of amidst my healing process. I had been tormented by so much. I was scarred emotionally from all of my relationships. These are times when we must be mindful and protective of our hearts. It always seems that when you are working to pull yourself together, temptation arises. At least that is how life unfolds for me. Along my journey to heal, I began a ritual of dating myself. I would go out to eat or to the movies alone. I was happy to do so and it allowed me opportunities to reflect and sit with my own thoughts.

I remember one weekend in particular, both my girls were with Ryan and Tamar and there was a restaurant that I had been dying to try. When I arrived, I requested a table right by the window because I could watch all of the people go by. The only problem was that they could see you too, but I didn't care; I had no one to impress. I began to skim the menu and found a few different options. The waitress came over to take my drink order and suggested that I take a little more time to review the menu, based on the recommendations that she made. From the distance, I heard a voice.

"Where have you been all my life beautiful?"

I recognized the voice, but I almost couldn't believe my ears. It was Desmond.

I could feel the hair on the back of my neck standing up because I was certain that when I turned around, he would look just as handsome as he always did. Just the sight of him did something to me. He reached for my hand and gestured for me to get up from the table and we embraced. As I stood there in his arms, I felt at home. I hadn't experienced anything so familiar in quite some time. I honestly didn't want him to let me go, but if we stood there any longer embracing, the rest of the patrons in the restaurant would begin to stare. I sat back down and invited him to sit with me. He had changed a little and added a little weight. He no longer had the long jerry curl as he wore a very professional, clean haircut. Even though he wasn't exactly as I had pictured him, his heart was what I had grown to love. I hadn't seen him since having the abortion and discovering that he had a girlfriend in the midst of our relationship. I should have been angry with him, but I couldn't find it within. Quite possibly, after spending so many years with bottled up anger and anxiety from the ordeal with Ryan and Tamar, I could only find peace. Besides, Desmond displayed that same charisma that had always drawn me in.   That night, we sat and talked for hours, catching up on life. He was, in fact, still married to the girlfriend that I called in my petty moment to tell her about the abortion. Even with all that had transpired, we shared something that was so real. It couldn't be denied. I learned that he was in Sacramento on business and he had indeed pursued the career that he strategized for. I was thrilled to know that he still possessed that same sense of direction for his life.

As the hours passed in the restaurant, it became apparent that neither of us wanted to say goodbye.

"What if you spend the weekend with me?" he asked.

"Whoa. The weekend? What about your wife? I mean, you are a married man. Trust me, after all that I have been through, I am not in the business of breaking up happy homes, and that's for sure."

"Well, what about homes that aren't happy? I haven't been happy for years. I've only stayed because of my son. I knew that letting you go was the biggest mistake of my life. I was too afraid to reach out to you. I feared that you hated me, but there is no way that I can let you ever go again. I am not willing to lose you a second time."

I don't know if he was lying or as desperate as he sounded, but I wanted to believe his profession of love. I needed to know that someone wanted me as deeply as I wanted them. He stood up and reached for my hand and he got in the car with me. He had arrived by taxi so there was nothing more to think about, except being together.

That night, the love we made rekindled everything between us. I could tell that he had learned a few new things since we were together when we were younger, but I'm not sure he was prepared for all that I now knew. Not to mention, I had so much sexual tension built up that I gave him a night he would never forget. In the middle of making love, he even told me that he regretted me not being the mother of his first child.

"Listen to me Rachel, I promise that if you can hold on until my son is eighteen and graduated from high school, I will give you all of the things that I should have given you before I let you walk out of my life. By that time, your divorce will have been finalized and there will be nothing standing in the way of us being together".

I rolled over and smiled from ear to ear. I was always like a schoolgirl when I was with him. He knew it. We spent the rest of the weekend making love and only came up for air and food. We ordered in because actually getting dressed and going to get food seemed like time that we could not afford to waste.

When Sunday arrived, I kissed him goodbye before he caught a taxi to the airport. I was sad to see him go. I wanted what we had just experience to last forever, but nothing was promised. I had learned that much over the years.

The following Monday after returning home from work, I checked the mail. "Bills, bills, and more bills," I said to myself. As I walked into the house and tossed the mail on the counter next to the sink, a white envelope that I hadn't noticed slid from under a Bed Bath and Beyond circular. It read "Child Support Services." I rolled my eyes and tossed the envelope back onto the counter. I refused to let Ryan and Tamar steal any more of my good moments. I had to decide if I was going to entertain the offer from Desmond. He still had a piece of my heart. I couldn't possibly predict how the story of our love would end because there were so many more chapters to be written. What I did know was that I wanted to be with him.

Desmond and I continued to speak on the phone and text multiple times per day, rekindling our romance. I can't lie and say that I didn't feel guilty, but he continued to assure me that he and his wife were living two separate lives and that they remained in the same house only for the sake of their son. I didn't want to stand in the way of the child in any way. I also continued with my self-care, because if I had learned nothing else, I was certain that nothing was guaranteed. I wanted to be with

Desmond, but I had also been hurt and was extremely leery of falling too hard for anyone.

The following weekend, I met some girlfriends at a local club to dance. Dancing was still something that I thoroughly enjoyed and I continued to make it a priority. That night, the club was exceptionally crowded. To my surprise, I even saw a few people that I had worked with at the real estate firm. When I hit the dance floor, the sound of the music vibrating through the walls sent energy right into my body. In those moments, I felt free and in touch with happiness. I raised my hands in the air and swayed to the tempo of the snare drum that was so crisp in the song. I felt another hand touch mine. I actually didn't enjoy dancing with people that I didn't know. I preferred to dance by myself or with my girlfriends. I prepared to turn around and tell whoever it was that I was not interested, but before I could, I felt his hand wrap around my waist and he pulled me closer to him. I recognized the fit of his body against mine, but it wasn't Desmond.

"You're so sexy when you move like that," he whispered in my ear.

My eyes lifted from looking down and I could feel the crooked smile on my face. Only Paxton could make me smile that way. I allowed him to caress me for a while. It felt natural. Moments later, I turned around and slapped him across the shoulder with my left hand. My right hand was resting on my hip because he was well overdue for me to give him a piece of my mind.

"Well, look what the cat drug in," I said sarcastically. "I haven't seen you since. . . well . . . you know."

"I do know and I think about you all the time. You know you were my best friend, right?"

"Boy, shut up. I've missed you too. Let's go catch up. Or is there someone else in here that I need to be aware of?"

"No, no one. I'm all yours."

We sat in the club and talked as if the music didn't exist. He told me all about how his life had been going and the new job that he had acquired. He also divulged that he and Ms. Waters were no longer an item. He then turned the spotlight on me. He had a way of doing that. It made you feel important because he could sit there listening for hours, allowing you to talk about yourself. I showed him pictures of the girls and he asked so many questions about McKenzie. It almost became offensive because the conversation turned completely in that direction, and I was unsure of why he was so interested.

"Good Lord, Paxton. How many questions are you going to ask me about McKenzie? You know that I am a good mom to my kids and that I love them both dearly. Why are you prying," I scolded.

"I'm so sorry. I'm not. It's just . . .It's just that —"

"'Just that' what? What are you trying to say?"

"I just really believe that McKenzie is not Ryan's daughter. I just know in my heart that McKenzie is mine."

"You are absolutely out of your mind. What in the hell are you insinuating? Do you know that I am in the midst of an ugly divorce and paternity test? I don't need any more drama in my life. Just stop it with your accusations. Just stop it."

I was fuming. How could any of what he was saying be true? Even though I was not sitting in church every day, I was still spiritually connected. There was no way that God would have allowed McKenzie to not be Ryan's daughter. How could that be possible? Ryan had been raising her and neither of us had any questions until that bitch Tamar came into the picture.

"Please! Just take a look at this picture. Please?" he begged.

"Fine, what picture?"

"Here, I've been dying to show you this anyway," he exclaimed.

"Wait, how did you get this picture of McKenzie? I mean, I don't even remember her having taken this."

"It's not McKenzie, it's my daughter Sylvia. The resemblance is startling isn't it?"   "Enough of it, Paxton. Enough of it. I should have known that this wasn't a good idea."

I stormed out of the club in both anger and desperation. When I stopped, just in front of the door, I noticed that my hand was shaking. Standing there, I realized that the timing of the envelope that I received, and the chance meeting with Paxton, were not by chance at all. Maybe in the midst of my cleansing, I also needed to address the paternity of McKenzie. I knew that even if I tried to sweep it under the rug, Tamar was not going to stop until she determined, once and for all, that McKenzie was not Ryan's. I had some long, hard decisions to make. What I did know was that the night that McKenzie was conceived, I had made love to both Ryan and Paxton. I had lied to myself all these years that it was not possible for her to belong to anyone other than Ryan. I never even allowed myself to believe it possible, but on this night, the truth was staring me in the face and I had to turn around and look back at it.

The past has a funny way of making surprise visits. By now, you'd think that I would have learned to pay close attention to the patterns of the past and I had, but sometimes you can get caught off guard. One thing that I know for sure is that when the storms of life rage, it's wise to find the shelter in a familiar place.

11: And Now, I'll do What's Best for Me

*"I'm sorry if this sounds harsh, but listen closely:
Let the muthafuckin bridge burn."*

Even if we wanted to, we don't have the power to predict the future. The only power that we have is to recognize patterns that determine how we will respond to what happens to us.

LIE #11: In Love, You Must Always Put Others First

As I sat in the courtroom staring the judge in the face, so many things that had been so hazed became clear to me. I had lived so long for everyone else. I carried the torch for my mother's deferred dreams and my father who fought demons, but lived as a rainbow painted with love. I had lived for moments to make my sisters proud and to develop a bond that could never be broken. I had lived for the kids that stood under the Nigga Tree, and the white friends who had welcomed me. I had lived for the pain of Peter and the desire of Desmond, and the passion with Paxton and the routine with Ryan. I had even lived for the temporary insanity that I endured at the hands of Ryan and Tamar. Up until now, I had not realized that there were only two reasons that I was alive: Talia and McKenzie. In that moment, staring at the face of a man elected to decide my fate, I realized that even my girls couldn't save me if I didn't exercise the power to save myself. I had lived for every damn body except myself. I can explain the mix or horror and happiness that I was overcome with. On the one hand, I was giving myself permission to be free from all of the uncertainty and pain that had plagued my life. On the other hand, I was mad as hell. I had given so many of my good years to some who were less than appreciative.

I could feel the beads of sweat building as I sat in angst. I could see Tamar peering at me from her seat on the other side of the lawyer, but I couldn't have cared less what she or anyone else thought. I had just experienced the epiphany of a lifetime.

I had lived so many years searching for love, but the heat in my body turned to chills running down my spine as I realized that I had never just lived my life for me. Life is about seizing every moment, of every hour, of every day. It's not possible for you to discover love when you don't love yourself. For so many years, I didn't love me. To love yourself is to learn with every single moment of life that you encounter. Most importantly, it becomes our responsibility to learn from the patterns of life that don't result in prosperity. In that moment, I could organize my thoughts more clearly than I ever had in any of the moments that I had spent alone trying to collect my thoughts.

Those thoughts were flowing like a waterfall and there was nothing I could do about it. I couldn't focus my attention in the courtroom because my mind was on overload. In that moment, I recognized my pattern with men. I realized that once I jumped out of a relationship, I got right back into another one. I used to feel like being in a relationship gave me a sense of purpose. I felt like if I wasn't in a relationship I wasn't a woman. After my relationships ended, I would get so lonely and so depressed. I never realized how much I depended on these men. I had a pattern of yearning to feel wanted and needed. I also recognized my patterns once I got the man. I recognized that when a guy met me, I was very much myself. I wouldn't always comb my hair, or if I wanted to burp and drink a beer, then I would burp and drink a beer. If I thought a man had unattractive habits, I would tell him. Over the years, men have seemed to find that intriguing, and yet, when I finally got the man, I changed. The laid back, speak it like I see it, take me as I am, woman, would turn and become a soft-spoken puppy. I would lose all of the raw and uncut personality, but it was because I was afraid of them leaving. I would do everything that I could to make them stay. I lived for not being alone. My eyes began to water, because sitting in the courtroom, feeling trapped with the decision of my fate in the hands of others, I recognized the error of my ways.

Sitting there, I also began to think about the patterns that affected my long career as a college student. I had always been ambitious, but every time I broke up with a guy, I would enroll in college. I did this for twelve years and never obtained a degree. My transcripts reflected how I would startup and dropout based on the ups and downs of my relationships. School was not hard for me, but the distraction of men was.

By now, it was obvious to everyone sitting in the court that I was crying. I'm certain that everyone believed that I was overcome with emotion because of the court proceedings. Nothing could have been further from the truth. I was emotionally moved because for the first time, I saw myself. I even recognized the good patterns that developed. In spite of all of the heartache, kids, pain, and identity crises, I never lost my job. I was always working and paying into my retirement. I smiled to myself because I felt proud of what I had been able to secure and the life that I had been able to create for my girls and me. If you're a women, you need to know that whatever you had the ability to hold on to, be proud of yourself. Whether it was your kids, your job, your home, your savings, hold onto it and tell your story as well. Sharing my story with you has been so draining for me, but it has allowed me to see how thankful I should be for the good days and the bad.

Sitting in that courtroom, I realized that the goal was not to chase a man for happiness, but to get an education to make my damn self happy. I realized that it is not wise to wait for Prince Charming. It is possible that he is out there, but he needs to come and find me, not the other way around. And while love was the last thing on my mind, I could still admit that I believed that there was a good, hard working, stable, intelligent man out there for me. If I am looking for him, he is not going to show up. It will be when I least expect it.

The most important thing that I recognized was that if you can't love yourself first, you couldn't love anyone else right. You must look inside and figure out if you like the person in the mirror.

I also recognized that I had a pattern of being good to people even when they weren't good back to me, and that was OK then, because I would have done anything in the name of love and trying to keep my family together. Time has a way of revealing that there are some circumstances that no longer serve us and those that can be toxic. When this is the case, we must learn to let go.

What I needed was to unlock the vault of lies that I had tucked so deeply inside my heart — the lies that I had witnessed, the lies from and within my own family, and even the lies that I had told myself. I needed to heal, not just usher the pain out the back door, and issue an invitation to new pain in the front window. Replacing pain with pain is a losing game. The true remedy would have been to repair my heart and discover a place of healing from the damage caused by failed relationships. It had taken me my whole life, up until that moment in the courtroom, to recognize that most valuable lesson.

Remember when I asked if love would ever love me back? I finally got my answer. It was a resounding yes! I began to ball my eyes out. There was of course a twist. I had to learn to love myself above all else first. I had searched for so long in the hopes that love would find me, when in fact, the greatest of it lived inside of me all along. I was just too caught up in a sea of lies to recognize it. The love that I have for my girls taught me the way that love works and how it replenishes itself when its stores are depleted. I would forever be grateful for having learned how to love from them.

There has never been, nor will there ever be, a question as to whether or not my girls will have the absolute best of what I can give them. That's mind, body, and soul. They are the greatest part of me. As I look back over my life, they are what I got right and I am tremendously proud of them. I have no regrets about my daughters.

I sat in the chair and forgave myself for anything that I could have been holding myself hostage for. I no longer deserved it. I freed my mind from whatever the results would be. They weren't relevant because no matter what they were, nothing would change the fact that I had walked in as Talia and McKenzie's mother and I would leave the courtroom as their mother still. I closed my eyes and sat back in my chair. I allowed my body to be as free as a soaring bird. I could hear the judge opening the envelope containing the results of McKenzie's paternity. I watched as the judge began to speak firmly. "In the case to establish paternity of McKenzie Alicia Suarez, it has been determined —"

I closed my eyes and said to myself, "And now I'll do what's best for me."

EPILOGUE

An Open Letter to My Girls,

Taylor you have been my ride or die from the very beginning. You have hung in there through all of my ups and downs. You have seen all the hurt and anger I have been through. Through all that you were always by my side and when I struggled and nobody was there to help us, you were whom I confided in. You saw me rob Peter to pay Paul and make ends meet. You were always my priority and I always provided for you, before I even provided for myself. It was important to me that you knew I was your biggest cheerleader in life and I still am. I wanted you and Madison to have something to remember me by when I'm long gone, which is why I founded "Foundation Tamara." That organization was simply to let you both know the importance of loving who you are and what you see in the mirror, and how to teach other young girls how to build themselves from within.

I also want you to understand how important it is not to conform to what "society" deems is correct. I love you so much; you are so beautiful and so smart. I want you to know you can do whatever it is you want to do in life. I have tried to be an example of that by starting a nonprofit and becoming a college graduate. You are on the right path. Continue to put God first and be still so that you can hear him speak to you. Remember to set your goals high and never let anyone tell you what you don't deserve, as they do not know your walk. Finally, thank you for giving me a beautiful grandson, Jermarie Pierre Johnson, Jr.

Madison, my little Maddy Cakes, boy, where do I begin? I can finally confess you are my favorite "youngest" daughter! You and Taylor have battled for so many years. I guess it all started the day she poured white out in your hair, covered your face in Vaseline, and swore you did it to yourself as she sat there with greasy hands. Then you retaliated by pouring a cup of red Kool-Aid in her face. As much as you two fight, I know you both love each other very much. You have been through so much from the time you were a young girl that my only hope was for you to blossom into a God-fearing, self-aware, grounded young women. If I have never said it loud enough, or the right way, I am saying it now publicly that I am so sorry for all the paternity issues you went through in your younger years. We all go through things in life, but I can't imagine how much pain that caused you and for that, I am sorry and ask for your forgiveness. I am so proud to see you navigate through life, graduating from college, and beginning your young adult career.

This novel I wrote, "Lies Men Tell," is something you two girls can relate to as it is loosely based on my life. Through each story in this book, I'm sure you can reflect on how I was able to bounce back from the deception of each man in my life. It is my hope that you two beautiful young ladies remember the importance of forgiveness and how forgiving really helps you to move forward in life. Without forgiveness, it is virtually impossible to heal. I have forgiven the men in my life that have wronged me and those that have lied and deceived me. For without them, there would be no story to tell. Always remember Madison and Taylor, God has a plan for you both. Do not judge your life by someone else's walk. You have your own path, your own destiny, and your own blessings. Never let anyone tell you what you can or cannot do. Never let the man in your life place limitations on your goals and dreams. Dream big and fearless. Don't allow fear to stop you from taking a step forward. Put God first, be honest, don't lie, don't do drugs, and pay your bills on time. You can do whatever it is you want and you can go wherever you want. Travel the world, visit other countries, learn new languages, and make new friends from other cultures because there is more to life than California. As a young woman, always be aware of your surroundings and know just who in your circle to keep an eye on. Embrace the "tadow theory." I taught you about that a long time ago. Don't tell all of your business, plans, and goals. Just do it, and then when it's done — tadow on they ass! People will always tell you why you shouldn't do something. The world out there is not going to stop for you. Stay hungry my loves. Go for it all, be determined, and remember you deserve it all and more.

Do me a favor, and learn to love each other unconditionally, as you two will always be family. Support each other and encourage each other to be great. My heart beats for the two of you. I love you so much and I dedicate this book to the both of you.

Love Always,

Mom

ABOUT THE AUTHOR

In the early 1990's, Raquel moved to Sacramento to begin life as a single mother. Today, as a mother of two daughters and a grandmother, she lives drama free. In 2005, Raquel established Foundation TAMARA to provide mentorship to young girls in Sacramento, California. Raquel feels that all young ladies deserve access to empowerment and inspiration. For more than ten years, Raquel has used writing as a form of therapy to cope with heartbreak and unhappiness as a result of failed relationships. Today, Raquel has transformed her journal into a series that is relatable to women around the world. Over the years, not only has Raquel learned the importance of self-love, but also making the most of life. Raquel Solomon was born and raised in Bakersfield, California, and is a proud graduate of Sacramento State University.

CONNECT WITH

RAQUEL SOLOMON

ON SOCIAL MEDIA

FACEBOOK: raqsolomon

INSTAGRAM: raqsolomon

TWITTER: @raqsolomon

WEBSITE: www.raqsolomon.com

EMAIL: raqsolomon@gmail.com

CPSIA information can be obtained
at www.ICGtesting.com
Printed in the USA
FSHW02n0618200918
52417FS